The Dynamics of Cross-Linguistic Instruction

Strategies for Building Biliteracy

Silvia Dorta-Duque de Reyes

To my husband Ricardo, and our children Andy, Ana, and Andrea,
for their unconditional love and support.

To educators who advocate for the shared goal of biliteracy.

Contents

Letter from the Author

Silvia Dorta-Duque de Reyes

Dear Teachers,

The early years of my career as a first-grade bilingual teacher were filled with joyous conversations with my students. The memories of their boundless curiosity and unique perspectives on life continue to bring a smile to my heart. These experiences drive my ongoing efforts to develop effective and meaningful teaching and learning strategies.

Together, my students and I explored concepts across various content areas, making connections to social science, science, mathematics, culture, and the visual and performing arts. Literature often served as a springboard for transformative dialogue about our lives and the social conditions that challenged our future. As we made linguistic and cultural connections, we realized the immense potential of our biliteracy. We proudly and frequently affirmed: *"¡El estudiante bilingüe vale por dos!"*

At that time, the rich cultural, linguistic, and intellectual capital of our language learners was often unappreciated and undervalued amid debates on the effectiveness of bilingual education. As a proud bilingual teacher, I felt an ethical and social responsibility to address and clarify misconceptions about biliteracy, and a moral imperative to affirm the benefits of bilingualism at personal, community, and national levels.

My praxis led me to embrace the deep historical, linguistic, and cultural connections between Spanish and English—languages that forged my identity. This involved questioning, studying, and organizing language and cultural constructs in ways that could be taught, explained, and negotiated by students.

Learning to read and write in alphabetic languages like English and Spanish follows universal principles, but the nuances of effective instruction for multilingual students require a deep understanding of the specific linguistic characteristics of each language. This book is crafted for educators, educational leaders, and administrators who are dedicated to fostering an environment where language learners can thrive through cross-linguistic transfer instruction.

In these pages, you will find a comprehensive resource filled with practical tools, strategies, and routines designed to help you plan, organize, and deliver effective cross-linguistic instruction. By addressing the similarities and differences across languages through an organized framework, this book aims to make the complex process of teaching two language systems both comprehensible and manageable.

It is a resource designed to deepen an understanding of skill transfer across languages, foster collaborative learning communities, and extend professional development opportunities. It integrates knowledge from various strands of literacy and biliteracy research, ensuring that standards-based teaching remains integral to student success in a biliteracy context.

The Dynamics of Cross-Linguistic Instruction: Strategies for Building Biliteracy is for all who recognize the urgency of maximizing and celebrating the linguistic potential of all students. Explicit teaching for cross-linguistic transfer promotes equity and ensures proficient language development leading to biliteracy. It facilitates instructional decision-making and lesson planning by providing effective cross-linguistic lessons, teaching strategies, and routines.

I am indebted to the profound scholars and researchers who pioneered and validated the efficacy of cross-linguistic transfer instruction, including Jim Cummins, Alma Flor Ada, Isabel Campoy, and Eleanor Thonis.

I am also grateful to experts in the field who have steadfastly helped pave the way: Jill Kerper Mora, Kathy Escamilla, Karen Beeman, and Cheryl Urow. My heartfelt acknowledgment goes out to colleagues Ana Applegate, Arlene Quintana-Rangel, Luz Elena Rosales, Izela Jacobo, Sandra Cejas, Lucia García, Jorge Cuevas Antillón, who believed in the efficacy of cross-linguistic transfer and collaborated to bring this work forward.

Last, but not least, a special thanks to Sera and Tom Reycraft of Benchmark Education, who center their business practices around what is best for teachers and students.

Warm regards,

–Silvia Dorta-Duque de Reyes

Putting It in Perspective

The Dynamics of Cross-Linguistic Instruction: Strategies for Building Biliteracy is the result of many tried-and-true lessons implemented at various grade levels and enhanced over the years. While the process of learning to read and write is the same across alphabetic languages, such as English and Spanish, effective instruction for multilingual learners must explicitly address the specific linguistic characteristics of the languages.

Who Should Use This Book

This book is written primarily for educators of multilingual students who want to implement cross-linguistic transfer instruction in their dual-language classrooms. It is also for educational leaders and administrators who are looking to support language learners with effective asset-oriented instruction. Whether you are multilingual or not, you still play a significant role in supporting, understanding, and teaching how two languages are connected, compared, and contrasted.

All educators can use this book as a practical resource to facilitate planning, organizing, and delivering cross-linguistic instruction. It provides step-by-step sample lessons, tools, strategies, and routines for successful implementation of cross-linguistic instruction.

How This Book Will Help

Teaching two languages, whether simultaneously or sequentially is a complex process. It demands understanding of how each language works and how they are similar and different. Using the language subsystems as an organizational framework, this book presents a rationale and process for addressing these similarities and differences in a way that is comprehensible and manageable for teaching and learning.

This resource includes features that will encourage educators to

- achieve a deeper understanding of constructs presented,
- create collaborating learning communities, and
- extend professional development opportunities.

The Dynamics of Cross-Linguistic Instruction applies the integration of knowledge from many strands of literacy and biliteracy research that inform best instructional practices. It reflects the understanding that standards-based teaching is integral to the success of students in a biliteracy instructional context. It serves as a practical guide that includes identifying opportunities, strategies, and routines for explicit instruction of cross-linguistic transfer skills.

How This Book Is Organized

The Dynamics of Cross-Linguistic Instruction is organized into two related sections: Pedagogy and Language Subsystems.

Part 1: Pedagogy

Chapter 1: What Is Cross-Linguistic Instruction?

Chapter 2: Language and Literacy Universals, Subsystems, and Relationships

Chapter 3: Designing Instruction Across Languages

Chapter 4: Assessment in a Biliteracy Context

Part 2: Language Subsystems

Chapter 5: Phonology

Chapter 6: Orthography

Chapter 7: Morphology

Chapter 8: Semantics

Chapter 9: Grammar and Syntax

Chapter 10: Pragmatics

The Dynamics of Cross-Linguistic Instruction

Part 1: Pedagogy

Pedagogical Considerations

Part 1 presents an overview of topics to provide a common and grounding understanding of important constructs related to instruction in two languages leading to biliteracy. Each of the four chapters in Part 1 addresses the foundational knowledge relating to cross-linguistic instruction.

Chapter 1 What Is Cross-Linguistic Instruction?

This introductory chapter provides a historical perspective and context grounded in theory and research as it begins to define cross-linguistic instruction. It includes working definitions of contrastive analysis, metacognitive skills, and metalinguistic skills. The chapter closes with a section on cultural parameters.

Chapter 2 Language and Literacy Universals, Subsystems, and Relationships

Chapter 2 explains how Language and Literacy Universals point us to the rules and characteristics that languages have in common. Also presented in this chapter are the language subsystems addressed in Part 2. The subsystems are used as a framework and springboard for planning transfer lessons. Cross-linguistic analysis for each subsystem occurs in tandem with core instruction. Terms for the variation of linguistic relationship between languages and how these affect approaches to teaching and learning are described.

Chapter 3 Designing Instruction Across Languages

This chapter turns our attention to the conditions that promote cross-linguistic transfer in bilingual and dual-language instructional settings. Creating a designated time for coherent instruction focusing on specific skills in context and across languages is presented. Steps for planning a standards-based cross-linguistic lesson are provided.

Chapter 4 Assessment in a Biliteracy Context

To conclude Part 1, the critical role of assessment in a bilingual classroom is emphasized. Considerations for the interpretation and analysis of data are discussed. The importance of establishing a management system that monitors student progress over time and across languages is also explained. A caveat relating to reading fluency assessments is addressed and appropriate fluency norms for Spanish reading fluency are provided.

Part 2: Language Subsystems

Language Subsystems as a Framework for Cross-Linguistic Instruction

Part 2 demonstrates the use of the language subsystems as an organizational framework to plan cross-linguistic transfer lessons. A solid understanding of these systems is critical when teaching cross-linguistic transfer. Languages are often studied in terms of their subsystems. These subsystems provide a way to describe, analyze, and study language components. As such, each subsystem is defined and described, and cross-linguistic connections and comparisons between English and Spanish are outlined. Each language subsystem is used as a point of reference for designing cross-linguistic instruction. Contrastive analysis for each of these subsystems occurs in tandem and correlated to instructional sequences in core programs. Sample lessons are presented across K–5 contexts in the "In Action" section of each chapter.

Chapter 5 Phonology

Chapter 5 describes cross-linguistic strategies that increase phonological awareness by comparing sounds across languages. This chapter stresses the importance of sound articulation and syllabication, explores the importance of similarity of learning conditions, and presents strategies and routines.

Chapter 6 Orthography

Chapter 6 presents teaching methodologies for cross-linguistic transfer of the Spanish and English sound-spelling systems. This chapter includes lessons for transferable and nontransferable sound-spelling relations. An assessment sequence for monitoring student progress toward negotiating the two sound-spelling systems is provided.

Chapter 7 Morphology

Chapter 7 examines the shared morphological features of Spanish and English. These languages share common Latin and Greek origins. Beyond word recognition and the study of cognates, the language-specific features and language universals relating to the distinct types of morphological units and how they apply to each language are addressed.

Chapter 8 Semantics

Chapter 8 explores the vocabulary and word relationships across English and Spanish. A variety of word-learning strategies for determining the meaning of unknown words in context are provided. Cultural variations as they relate to words, phrases and idioms, and other language structures are analyzed.

Chapter 9 Grammar and Syntax

Chapter 9 includes strategies for comparing grammatical constructs relating to sentence structure and functions of words within a sentence. Word order reflects language norms and thought patterns in any given language. Therefore, strategies for the analysis of implied cultural connotations and implications are provided.

Chapter 10 Pragmatics

Chapter 10 dives deeper into pragmatics. Communicative competence, which refers to the ability to use language successfully in a variety of social and academic interactions, is explored. This chapter conveys how context contributes to meaning and how language manifests through text structures. Practical strategies that emphasize the relationship between pragmatics and cross-cultural competence are highlighted.

Our journey begins...

El camino se hace al andar...

Please know that this book you are holding was intended and written for you—and the teaching and learning possibilities you are envisioning. Know that we share the commitment of expanding the joys and advantages of multilingualism to all.

I hope this book will serve you as a companion for exploring the depth and beauty of language, culture, and identity. I hope it will promote critical thinking and foster the power of biliteracy as you and your students engage in transformative dialogue and self-discovery. I hope that this book helps us embrace the implementation of cross-linguistic transfer instruction.

As you venture on this learning journey, may your steps be filled with courage, enthusiasm, passion, and compassion. Finally, know that you and your contributions as an educator are deeply appreciated and indispensable for society, democracy, and global understanding.

Pedagogía

Part 1

Pedagogy

Part 1 explores key concepts related to instruction in two languages that ultimately lead to biliteracy. Each of the four chapters in Part 1 delves into the essential aspects of cross-linguistic instruction, providing a comprehensive exploration of foundational knowledge in this area. Through these chapters, readers will gain insights into the principles, strategies, and practices essential for effective cross-linguistic instruction in a bilingual context—which lays the groundwork for students' successful biliteracy development.

Chapter 1

What Is Cross-Linguistic Instruction?

"Our understanding of what constitutes biliteracy instruction is dynamic and ever evolving, but the effectiveness of explicit cross-linguistic transfer instruction can no longer be denied."

"Nuestro entendimiento sobre lo que constituye la enseñanza de la alfabetización bilingüe es dinámico y está en constante evolución, pero lo que ya no se puede negar es la eficacia de la enseñanza explícita de la transferencia interlingüística".

–Silvia Dorta-Duque de Reyes, 2024

Behind every public policy, research study, assessment instrument, or instructional strategy is a set of assumptions. These assumptions are articulated in the academic world and validated through rigorous research as theories. As reflective practitioners, we base our program designs and instructional practices on a solid theoretical knowledge base and rigorous research.

Therefore, the instructional practices that we embrace and make our own must go beyond ideological biases and adhere to research criteria that determine their effectiveness. This chapter explores the foundational research base related to cross-linguistic transfer that can be applied in dual-language education for effective classroom instruction.

In This Chapter

- Foundational Theory and Research
- Transfer and Retention of Learning
- Cross-Linguistic Transfer
- Building Biliteracy: An Asset-Based Approach

Foundational Theory and Research

James Cummins (1981) explains the transference of knowledge and skills from one language to another through the Linguistic Interdependence Hypothesis. With this theory, he proposes that the proficiencies developed in two languages are interdependent, meaning they rely on each other and support cognitive processes and comprehension of complex ideas.

He uses the metaphor of a dual iceberg to illustrate that although the surface features of two languages differ, at a deeper level the proficiencies developed in the two languages represent the same knowledge base.

Above the surface are the Basic Interpersonal Communication Skills (BICS); because these skills are often culturally bound, they are depicted as above the water surface.

Key Terms

BICS: Basic Interpersonal Communication Skills: social language used in every day conversation.

CALP: Cognitive Academic Language Proficiency: language needed for academic success.

CUP: Common Underlying Proficiency: a common underlying central operating system that supports shared cognitive and linguistic processes across languages.

According to this theory, children develop these Basic Interpersonal Communication Skills as they are exposed to a second language in social contexts, such as interactions with friends or family members who speak the second language. These skills are often developed through implicit learning and do not typically require explicit instruction.

Cognitive Academic Language Proficiency (CALP) refers to the language skills needed for academic achievement, such as understanding complex texts, writing essays, and engaging in critical thinking. CALP can be shared across languages and includes the deeper levels of cognitive processing and thinking skills such as analysis, synthesis, and evaluation.

The Common Underlying Proficiency (CUP) represents a common underlying central operating system where cognitive skills in one language support learning in another language. Both languages are outwardly distinct but are supported by shared concepts and knowledge derived from learning and experience as well as by the cognitive and linguistic abilities of the learner.

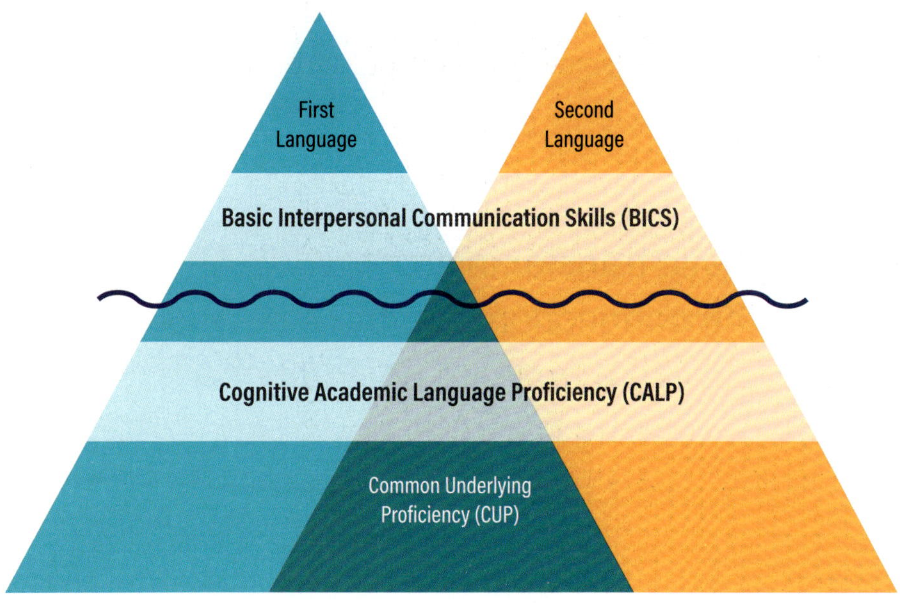

Linguistic Interdependence Hypothesis Iceberg Model (Cummins, 1981)

This Common Underlying Proficiency between a first and second language promotes the development of cognitive academic skills. This system refers to the interdependence of concepts, skills, and linguistic knowledge found in the central processing system in the human brain. Cummins (1981) proposes that in this central processing system, the human brain integrates all language knowledge.

This integration relates to cross-linguistic instruction because it proposes that language knowledge can transfer from one language to another. In other words, the metacognitive (ability to think about thinking and learning) and metalinguistic (ability to think about how language works) skills are shared understandings between a person's first language and any additional languages learned.

In addition, Cummins's (1981) theory suggests that the more developed a person's metacognitive and metalinguistic skills are in their first language, the more quickly they can develop proficiency in additional languages. Cross-linguistic transfer instruction promotes the connection, comparison, and contrast between a first and an additional language by making common underlying proficiencies overt to students.

"Cross-linguistic transfer instruction promotes the connection, comparison, and contrast between a first and an additional language by making common underlying proficiencies overt to students."

Research affirms that explicit teaching for cross-linguistic transfer enhances students' knowledge and control of linguistic resources across languages.

Key Research

Research from August, Calderón, and Carlo (2002) affirms Cummins's (1981) hypothesis. They found that a positive effect of cross-linguistic transfer in English and Spanish exists for phonemic segmentation and blending skills, letter identification, and word reading skills. This research demonstrates the specific application of Cummins's hypothesis to the cross-linguistic transfer of literacy skills across Spanish and English.

In a subsequent study, the researchers pointed out that to reap the potential benefits of this linguistic interdependence, instruction must focus directly on explicit teaching for transfer (August et al., 2002). When cross-linguistic transfer is taught explicitly, students engage in connecting, comparing, or contrasting the concepts and skills already known in one language to learn the other. It cannot be assumed that language learners at the emerging stages of language and literacy development have the metalinguistic and metacognitive awareness to discern the similarities and differences between two language systems.

Beyond the Linguistic Interdependence Hypothesis, research affirms that explicit teaching of cross-linguistic transfer enhances students' knowledge and control of linguistic resources across languages (Bialystok, 2007; Howard et al., 2018).

Learn More

Cummins, J. (1981). The role of primary language development in promoting educational success for language minority students. In C. F. Leyba (Ed.), with California State Department of Education, Office of Bilingual Bicultural Education, *Schooling and language minority students: A theoretical framework.* (3rd ed., 2005, pp. 3–49). Evaluation, Dissemination and Assessment Center, California State University. files.eric.ed.gov/fulltext/ED249773.pdf (pp. 16–62)

August, D. A., Calderón, M., & Carlo, M. (2002). *Transfer of skills from Spanish to English: A study of young learners* [Report for practitioners, parents and policy makers]. Center for Applied Linguistics. https://www.cal.org/acquiringliteracy/pdfs/skills-transfer.pdf

Gradual Release of Responsibility

The Gradual Release of Responsibility (GRR) model is a teaching framework that directly supports the transfer of learning by progressively shifting the responsibility for learning from the teacher to the student.

This method ensures that students develop the independence and confidence needed to apply their learning in new and diverse contexts. The GRR model consists of four key phases, each designed to scaffold the transfer of learning:

- modeling by teacher
- guided practice
- collaborative practice
- independent practice

Transfer and Retention of Learning

All educators, regardless of the grade level or subject they teach, share common educational goals. The first goal is that of transfer of learning. Grant Wiggins (2012) defined transfer of learning as the ability to apply knowledge and skills learned in one context to different, novel situations. Wiggins emphasized that transfer is the ultimate goal of education, and that real learning is demonstrated when students can use their knowledge in unpredictable, real-world circumstances and not just repeat memorized information in familiar or testing conditions.

There are two important stages of transfer of learning:

1. **Teacher to students:** Occurs during the learning process, often using instructional strategies like Gradual Release of Responsibility;

2. **Student to real-world application:** Happens when knowledge or skills are used in real-life situations, which demonstrates retention and independent application.

However, transfer of learning is not the mere plugging in of a previously learned knowledge or skill, but rather the result of transfer by design: continuously providing scaffolded learning opportunities for students to prove understanding and make deeper meaning by moving their understanding (Heick, 2014).

The second goal is retention. Retention refers to the ability to remember and retrieve information. When we retain information, we store it in our long-term memory and can access it later when needed. Retention is important for learning because it allows us to build on our existing knowledge and skills, to apply them later in new learning and in different contexts.

Retention of learning requires that students remember what they have learned, whereas transfer of learning requires students not only to remember, but also to make sense of and flexibly apply what they have learned (Anderson & Krathwohl, 2001).

Retention and transfer are deeply connected. Strong retention means students have a solid foundation of knowledge that they can build on and apply in new contexts. Without retention, transfer is impossible because the student will not have anything to recall or apply.

Weak learning, characterized by superficial understanding, is unlikely to be retained by students and, as a result, cannot be transferred to new or real-life situations. Educators must focus on strengthening both the quality of their instruction and the depth of student understanding to ensure that learning is retained and can be transferred to new contexts.

Both retention and transfer are essential to cross-linguistic transfer instruction. Educators can help students build a solid foundation of knowledge and skills in one language, then explicitly teach how to apply that knowledge and skill in the partner language.

Example

Teacher to Students

In math class, the teacher ensures that students have acquired the knowledge needed to learn the value of coin by modeling and providing opportunities for guided and collaborative practice using manipulatives and scaffolded learning. Three weeks later, most students score high marks on their unit assessment, demonstrating they have learned and retained the information.

Student to Real-World Application

A student from that class runs an errand for his mother. He goes to the store where he discerns how much to spend to buy vegetables for his mother, hoping he will have money left to purchase a pack of baseball cards.

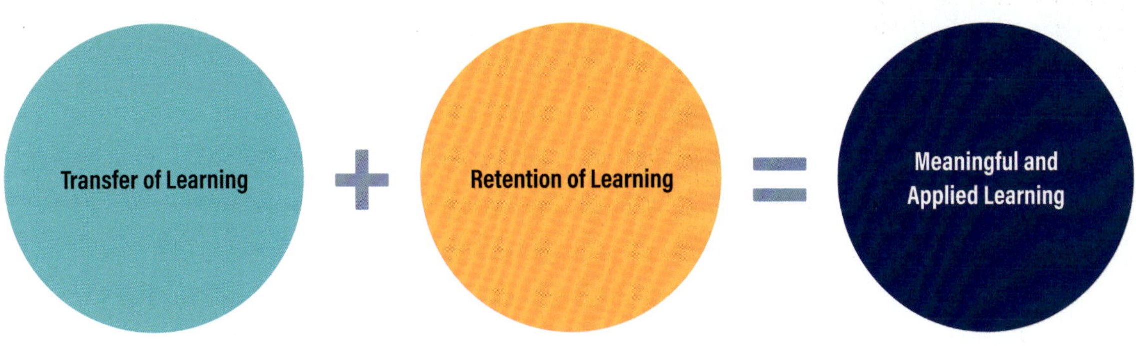

Cross-Linguistic Transfer

Transfer and retention are important in all learning, but they are especially important in dual-language learning contexts. Language transfer and retention are most evident and critical as those seeking to learn a new language apply what they already know in their first language to build proficiency and literacy in their new language.

Cross-linguistic transfer is the application of linguistic features, language structures, knowledge, and skills from one language to another (Thonis, 1983). This transfer can be general or specific.

- **General skill transfer:** This occurs when a learner can generalize knowledge acquired in one language to a different language. General skills are usually transferable so they can be taught in either or both languages. An example of general skill transfer is understanding that print represents speech in Spanish and English.

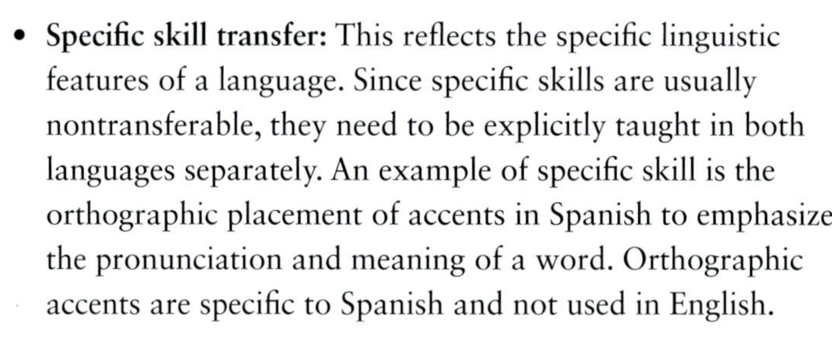

- **Specific skill transfer:** This reflects the specific linguistic features of a language. Since specific skills are usually nontransferable, they need to be explicitly taught in both languages separately. An example of specific skill is the orthographic placement of accents in Spanish to emphasize the pronunciation and meaning of a word. Orthographic accents are specific to Spanish and not used in English.

Eleanor Thonis (1983) explained that learners generalize from their experiences and apply what they know to the new learning. The strength and mastery of the original learning greatly influences the extent of success in the new learning. In other words, weak learning in one language does not transfer to the other.

Explicit teaching builds deeper knowledge of how each language works.

Some students recognize similarities and differences between languages on their own, making an intuitive leap in applying what they already know to the new language (Bruner, 1960, 1966). However, it cannot be assumed that all students will make this intuitive leap without a reasonable and orderly sequence of learning.

Therefore, rather than leaving this linguistic transfer up to chance, it can be intentionally and strategically taught. Explicit teaching for cross-linguistic transfer builds a deeper knowledge of the unique features of each language and how each language works. This is accomplished with contrastive analysis, which intentionally provides a comprehensible connection between languages. As teachers implement explicit cross-linguistic instruction, students learn to think strategically and develop the metacognitive and metalinguistic skills needed for proficient biliteracy.

Contrastive Analysis

Contrastive analysis is the systematic study of two languages that seeks to identify their specific structural differences and similarities. When students engage in contrastive analysis, they are comparing, contrasting, and making connections between languages. Contrastive analysis unveils how the language-specific features of two languages are similar and different. Central to the process of contrastive analysis is identifying how language-specific features are formed and used in each language. This process helps to determine which features are transferable or nontransferable.

When teachers understand the similarities and differences between the two languages, they can plan and deliver instruction that facilitates and supports cross-linguistic transfer. For this reason, Part 2 of this book dives into the language subsystems as a framework for teaching cross-linguistic transfer across Spanish and English. To start, here is a simple example of contrastive analysis:

Example

When studying language conventions for punctuation with first graders, a teacher points out that in both Spanish and English all sentences begin with a capital letter and end with a period.

The teacher elicits students' selective attention during explicit cross-linguistic transfer instruction to point out that in Spanish, exclamation marks and question marks are placed at the beginning and the end of an exclamatory statement or a question. On the other hand, in English, exclamation marks and question marks are placed only at the end of an exclamatory statement or a question.

Metacognitive Skills

Metacognition is the awareness of one's own thought processes. It is a higher-order thinking skill that involves being aware of oneself as a thinker and a learner. By knowing their thinking and learning processes, students understand content knowledge, learning tasks, and what learning strategies work best for them. Students become self-directed learners, able to generalize, organize, and regulate their learning. Metacognitive skills are transferable across languages. Here are a few examples of metacognitive skills:

- asking questions
- visualizing
- determining text importance
- making inferences
- summarizing
- synthesizing
- making connections
- predicting
- using monitoring strategies

Key Terms

Contrastive Analysis: The systematic study of two languages that seeks to identify their specific structural differences and similarities.

Metacognitive Skills: The ability to think about one's own thinking processes.

> "Metacognitive skills are transferable across languages."

When explicitly teaching cross-linguistic transfer, teachers guide students to become metacognitive thinkers by helping them understand how they are processing information. A good example is a think-aloud. During a think-aloud, teachers model thinking aloud and invite students to think about their thinking and explain their thought processes.

Teachers can also promote metacognitive skills by asking students to describe details present in illustrations that are not explicitly stated in the text, or to predict an outcome based on a sequence of prior events. When teaching cross-linguistic transfer, teachers explicitly point out that we apply these thinking processes and skills in the same way when reading in each language.

Example

To summarize a fable in a Spanish-language Kindergarten class, the teacher uses a 4-picture diagram. The teacher invites students to add key details from the story to each square of the diagram. The teacher numbers each square to indicate the sequence and provides students with key transitional words to facilitate the summary-retell. After the teacher models the retell, students use the 4-picture diagram to retell the story to a partner. The teacher deliberately prompts metalinguistic skills by asking: *¿Creen que en inglés también se usan palabras que indican la secuencia de un cuento? (Do you think we can retell stories in English using sequence words?)*

During English time, the teacher reads a different fable in English and also uses a 4-picture diagram—providing a similarity of learning conditions to facilitate cross-linguistic transfer and summary-retell in English. She explains to students that in both Spanish and English, a story is summarized using the key details and the sequence of the story. The teacher points out the correlating transition words in English and explains that these words have the same function in Spanish: they help connect one idea to the next. Both lessons promote students' metalinguistic skills by explaining that reading skills and strategies are the same in English and Spanish.

Primero, *la liebre organizó una carrera.* ***Después,*** *salió corriendo rápido, dejando atrás a la tortuga.* ***Entonces,*** *confiada, se durmió mientras la tortuga seguía avanzando.* ***Finalmente,*** *la tortuga llegó primera a la meta.*

First, *the lion wanted to eat the mouse.* ***Then,*** *he let the mouse go free.* ***Next,*** *the lion got caught in a trap, so the mouse chewed the rope to free him.* ***Finally,*** *they became friends forever.*

Metalinguistic Skills

Metalinguistic skills are the ability to use language to think, talk, and reflect upon language itself. Metalinguistic awareness involves a learner consciously reflecting or thinking about how language works and how much that learner can monitor their accuracy and self-correct. In other words, students demonstrate the ability to analyze, understand, and manipulate language as a system. When students engage in cross-linguistic learning, they discover how language works by comparing one language to the other as they generate and act on this internal feedback. There are four broad categories of metalinguistic skills.

Metalinguistic Categories	Definition
Phonological Awareness	The ability to think about and use phonemes
Semantic Awareness	The ability to think about word meanings and relationships
Syntactic Awareness	The ability to think about language
Pragmatic Awareness	The ability to use language appropriately according to purpose, task, and audience

Metalinguistic awareness is critical if cross-linguistic transfer is to occur.

Some examples of metalinguistic skills are:

- being aware that language structure can be manipulated
- being aware of language play, sarcasm, and jokes
- being aware that language has the potential for multiple meanings
- understanding the distinct parts of speech and their functions
- recognizing and using figurative language
- explaining the meaning of words and phrases
- analyzing the structure of sentences and paragraphs
- understanding the nuances of different dialects and accents

Teachers also facilitate the development of metalinguistic skills and awareness by providing students the opportunities to engage in comparing the similarities and differences between their native language and their new language.

> "Metalinguistic skills are the ability to use language to think, talk, and reflect upon language itself."

Example

When conducting a Spanish word study lesson, the teacher points out that the prefix **tele-**, comes from the Latin language and it means "at a distance." The teacher provides several examples of words with **tele-** prefixes as she explains the meaning of each word: *teléfono, telégrafo, televisor, telescopio.*

The teacher explains that Latin is the base language for many modern Romance languages including Spanish. English, on the other hand, is a Germanic language, but it has borrowed and continues to borrow Latin prefixes, roots, and suffixes to form academic words, as well as governmental and scientific terms.

The teacher explains that cognates are words in two languages that share a similar meaning, spelling, and pronunciation, and asks students to compare and contrast words in Spanish and English with the **tele-** prefix.

Students discover that they are all cognates because they have a common linguistic origin—in other words, they derive from the same ancestral language. The teacher affirms that many words in Spanish and English are cognates.

As an extension activity, the teacher encourages students to look for other words with the Latin prefixes **tele-** in both Spanish and English.

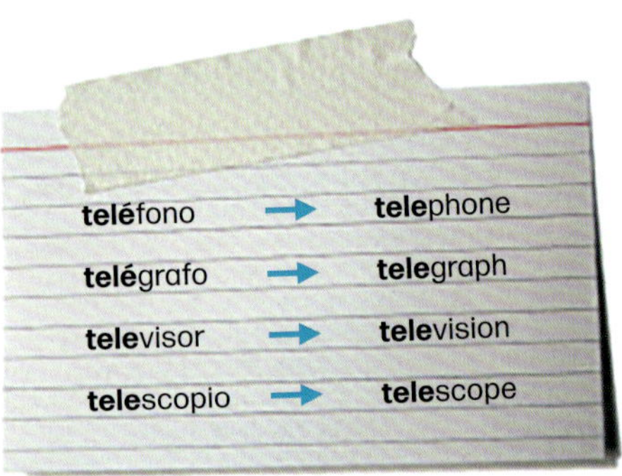

By intentionally providing a comprehensible connection between languages, explicit teaching for transfer promotes metalinguistic skills and awareness as students think about the languages they are using and learning. Explicit teaching for cross-linguistic transfer promotes metacognitive and metalinguistic skills as students are taught to think about the languages they are learning and using.

Building Biliteracy: An Asset-Based Approach

Asset-based instruction for biliteracy recognizes and values the linguistic and cultural backgrounds of students and views their home language and culture as an asset that should be nourished and developed rather than as a deficit or an obstacle to learning.

The goals of an asset-based approach are to build biliteracy by focusing on student's strengths while students develop their linguistic resources and to promote a healthy bilingual and bicultural identity.

Educators foster a supportive learning environment that values diversity by:

- incorporating culturally relevant topics, materials, and activities
- encouraging students to leverage their linguistic resources to negotiate meaning
- giving students agency

Biliteracy provides individuals with a unique set of skills to promote personal, academic, and social success.

The Value and Benefits of Biliteracy

Being bilingual enables us to be twice as efficient, useful, and generous. Recognizing and affirming the value of bilingualism and multiculturalism is an essential and integral aspect of dual-language education. By instilling in students the cognitive, academic, social, and personal benefits of becoming bilingual, we contribute to their overall personal development, increasing their motivation and perseverance.

Educators have numerous ways to foster bilingualism by involving students in affirming its value. Activities such as student-created posters, poetry, narratives, PowerPoints, videos, surveys, songs, and speeches are effective in promoting bilingualism throughout the school and community. Furthermore, there are many benefits of biliteracy and becoming a biliterate person.

Cognitive: aids with problem-solving and decision-making skills

Academic: promotes academic performance in content areas and advances language development

Economic: provides flexibility in a global economy

Cultural: advances cultural awareness and understandings

Social: promotes diverse interpersonal relationships

An asset-based approach to biliteracy also promotes cross-cultural communication and understanding. Individuals who are proficient in more than one language are better able to understand and appreciate diverse perspectives and cultural practices, which can foster empathy, respect, and collaboration across cultural and linguistic boundaries.

In today's globalized world, being bilingual or multilingual can provide individuals with a competitive advantage in the job market and enhance their cultural and social experiences. Most of all, biliteracy is an asset that helps students to maintain a strong connection to their families and cultural heritage.

Culturally and Linguistically Responsive Instruction

Related to the asset-based approach is culturally and linguistically responsive instruction (CLRI). This framework recognizes that students bring their own unique experiences, knowledge, and skills to the classroom, and seeks to build on these assets to create a more inclusive and effective learning environment.

Teachers seek to build positive relationships with their students and create a supportive learning environment that fosters collaboration and mutual respect. Accomplishing this requires ongoing assessment and reflection on student learning. Teachers use data and feedback to inform their teaching and create learning experiences responsive to their students' needs and interests.

> Students bring their own unique experiences, knowledge, and skills to the classroom.

Responsive instruction involves a variety of strategies such as:

- building relationships with students and their families
- incorporating cultural diversity into the curriculum
- using strategies that promote collaboration such as cooperative learning, group work, academic conversations, and collective storytelling
- supporting language development by providing instruction and tasks appropriate for students' proficiency levels
- recognizing home language as an asset and a springboard to learning
- valuing bilingualism and multilingualism
- providing equitable opportunities for students to show their learning

When teaching cross-linguistic transfer, a responsive approach to instruction is essential because it recognizes the importance of students' cultural and linguistic backgrounds in the learning process.

CLRI can also help to break down barriers that may impede cross-linguistic transfer. For example, students who feel disconnected from the curriculum or the classroom environment may be less likely to transfer skills and knowledge across languages. CLRI can support cross-linguistic transfer by providing instruction that is relevant and meaningful to students' cultural and linguistic backgrounds. Like cross-linguistic transfer instruction, CLRI incorporates strategies that draw on students' language, cultural experiences, and existing funds of knowledge to support learning.

Funds of Knowledge

The phrase "funds of knowledge" refers to the knowledge and skills that each of us possess from our everyday experiences and cultural background. When applied to instruction, the concept of funds of knowledge deliberately recognizes and values the knowledge and experiences that students and their families bring to a classroom community of learners.

These funds of knowledge often come from various sources:

- cultural traditions
- family history
- work experiences
- hobbies
- community involvement
- prior schooling

Teachers can tap into and include the knowledge and experiences of their students and their families to create a rich, relevant, and engaging learning community.

Pause and Reflect

What funds of knowledge do your students bring to the classroom?

In your own words, how does grounding instruction in students' funds of knowledge promote cross-linguistic transfer?

Home-school connections are essential for academic success.

> Cross-linguistic transfer instruction includes the comparison and contrasting of funds of knowledge in a community of learners.

Dr. Alma Flor Ada (1990) reminds us that strong bonds between home and school are essential if the educational process is to be effective. She suggests ways to involve parents meaningfully through

- direct interaction and dialogue,
- activities that parents and their children can easily carry out at home, and
- integrating parents' funds of knowledge as part of the academic curriculum.

Cross-linguistic transfer instruction includes the comparison and contrasting of funds of knowledge in a community of learners. It harvests this abundant knowledge as it explores the dynamics across culture, knowledge, and language.

Culture, Knowledge, and Language

Culture, knowledge, and language are deeply intertwined and interconnected. Culture influences the way knowledge is constructed and shared, and language is the primary tool through which culture and knowledge are transmitted. Together, culture, knowledge, and language are crucial for effective communication and promoting cultural awareness, diversity, and equity.

- Culture refers to the shared values, beliefs, customs, practices, and social behaviors of a group of people. It shapes the way people understand and interpret the world around them and provides a framework for organizing and communicating knowledge.
- Knowledge refers to the information, skills, and understandings that people acquire through education, experience, and observation. It is constructed and shared within cultural contexts and is often transmitted through language.
- Language is a system of symbols and rules used for communication. It enables people to express their thoughts, feelings, and experiences and to share knowledge and culture. Language is an integral part of culture, and it reflects and reinforces cultural values, beliefs, and practices.

Cultural parameters refer to the values, beliefs, and customs that define the boundaries of a particular culture. These parameters provide a framework for understanding and interpreting cultural practices, behaviors, and communication.

Cultural parameters vary widely across diverse cultures and can have a significant impact on how we interact with others and navigate social situations. For example, in some cultures, direct eye contact is considered a sign of respect and engagement, while in other cultures it may be considered to be a sign of aggression or disrespect.

Cultural parameters can be particularly important in teaching and learning. Educators need to be aware of the cultural values and beliefs of their students and the communities they serve, while creating learning experiences that are sensitive to those values and beliefs to promote cross-cultural understanding.

Educators who share a vision of biliteracy and multiculturalism encourage and invite students to connect, compare, and affirm cultural parameters.

Conclusion

Cross-linguistic transfer instruction is a research-based practice with proven benefits: improved language learning because students are explicitly taught how to build on their linguistic resources; increased confidence and motivation because students' known language is valued and used as a resource for learning; and increased cultural awareness and sensitivity.

In addition, the process of analyzing how two languages work by connecting, comparing, and contrasting features of both languages promotes cognitive development and critical thinking skills.

Key Takeaways

Decades of theory and research support the benefits of explicitly teaching for cross-linguistic transfer.

Contrastive analysis is the process of connecting, comparing, and contrasting language features across languages.

Cross-linguistic transfer engages students' funds of knowledge and linguistic and cultural assets to build metacognitive, metalinguistic, and multicultural skills.

Chapter 2

Language and Literacy Universals, Subsystems, and Relationships

> "El lenguaje no es sólo una llave para abrir puertas al entendimiento, sino también una poderosa herramienta para cambiar el mundo".
>
> *"Language is not only a key to open doors of understanding but also a powerful tool to change the world."*
>
> –Ada & Campoy, 2023b

Language and literacy universals are features or patterns found in all human languages. These are important because they help us understand the basic principles and structures that underlie all languages. By identifying and studying these commonalities, we can gain insights into the relationships that exist across languages.

Additionally, language and literacy universals can be used to organize cross-linguistic transfer instruction to develop effective language teaching and learning strategies. They can also inform our understanding of the cultural and social contexts in which language is used and help us to appreciate the diversity and richness of human communication. This chapter explores these linguistic relationships as they relate to English and Spanish.

In This Chapter

Language and Literacy Universals

Language universals and literacy universals are two important concepts to understand when teaching multiple languages simultaneously. Language universals are about how language works. Literacy universals are about learning to read and write in alphabetical languages. Both types of universals are learned and applied as biliteracy develops.

Students learn language and literacy universals as their biliteracy develops.

Language Universals

Languages are rule-governed systems. This means that all languages follow a set of rules. Each language also contains contrasting features specific to that language. Some languages have rules and characteristics in common. Languages originating from the same language family, meaning they have similar origins, tend to share quite a few similarities. When contrasting languages with dissimilar origins, more differences are typically evident. Regardless of a language's origin, however, all languages have certain rules that provide the structures for communicating meaning. These rules that all languages share are called language universals. They are the "global" features of languages. Language universals include:

- All languages have sounds.
- All languages have words that carry meaning.
- All languages have grammatical structures and word order.
- All languages have distinct patterns used in social interaction.

Learn More

Mora, J. K., & Dorta-Duque de Reyes, S. (in press). *Biliteracy and cross-cultural teaching: A framework for standards-based transfer instruction in dual language programs.* Brookes Publishing.

Thonis, E. (1983). *The English-Spanish connection.* Santillana USA.

Literacy Universals

Literacy universals are the common characteristics of written languages. They relate specifically to the correlation between speech and print. They refer to the basic skills and knowledge that are common across all cultures and societies when reading and writing, such as the ability to recognize and interpret letters and symbols. Literacy universals include:

- the importance of oral traditions and storytelling
- the use of symbols to represent sounds
- the development of writing systems
- the use of reading materials

Both language and literacy universals are essential for cross-linguistic instruction. Together they show us how a language works and how encoding/decoding of meaning occurs. It should be noted that language universals include components or subsystems that work together in consistent and predictable ways to produce meaning. Next, we will take a closer look at the language subsystems and how they relate to cross-linguistic instruction.

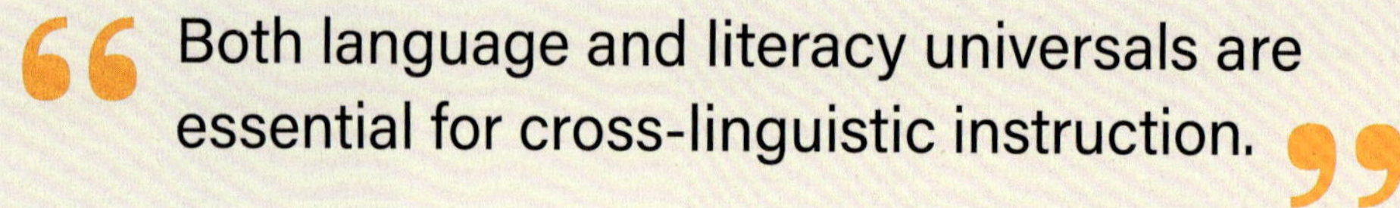

Language Subsystems

The subsystems of language are an organizational framework from which to plan transfer lessons centered in the similarities or differences between two languages (Dorta-Duque de Reyes, 2005). The language subsystems are:

Phonology
Orthography
Morphology
Semantics
Grammar and Syntax
Semantics
Pragmatics

These subsystems can be connected, compared, and contrasted across languages. Therefore, teachers can plan and organize a cross-linguistic transfer lesson by focusing instruction on language universals and language-specific features within the different subsystems. Contrastive analysis across these subsystems occurs in correlation with the instructional sequence of the core programs and at a designated bridging or cross-linguistic time.

Key Terms

Literacy Universals: The common characteristics of written languages (e.g., the use of symbols to represent sounds).

Language Subsystems: An organizational framework of language components that support transfer instruction.

Teachers in biliteracy contexts utilize their knowledge of the subsystems and components of language in teaching for cross-linguistic transfer. They integrate cross-linguistic instruction as they implement their core instruction. This table outlines the metalinguistic skills and language universals that relate to each subsystem.

Subsystems	Metalinguistic Skill	Language Universal
Phonology	Phonological Awareness	All alphabetic languages have sounds.
Orthography	Orthographic Awareness	Sounds are represented by letters that make up words.
Morphology	Morphological Awareness	Words have meaningful parts and can be compounded.
Semantics	Semantic Awareness	Words have meaning and represent concepts.
Syntax	Syntactic Awareness	Words have a predictable order in a sentence.
Grammar	Grammatical Awareness	Words have varied functions in a sentence.
Pragmatics	Sociocultural Awareness	Language use varies depending on social and cultural context.

(Dorta-Duque de Reyes & Mora, 2011)

English-Spanish Cross-Linguistic Relationships

For the purposes of this book, and for the benefit of educators seeking to address the needs of the millions of multilingual learners in Spanish/English dual-language programs, the cross-linguistic relationship between English and Spanish will be our primary focus.

Variations between languages determine the extent to which prior knowledge and learning experiences facilitate new learning. Thonis (1983, 2005) defined these variations in terms of linguistic relationships. Theorists refer to these variations in influence as positive transfer, partial transfer, negative transfer, or zero transfer.

Linguistic variations affect the extent to which prior knowledge facilitates new learning.

Positive Transfer

Positive transfer occurs when the known language skills facilitate the acquisition of the new language. For example, English and Spanish share many of the same alphabetic symbols (letters). Students who know the Spanish alphabet can positively transfer this knowledge to English. Skills that transfer in both the general and in the specific sense are examples of positive transfer.

Cognates are a prime example of positive transfer. Observe how the known language (Spanish) is mirrored and easily comprehensible in the learned language (English). These similarities promote positive transfer of learning.

Spanish	English
presidente	president
transformación	transformation

Many reading skills have a positive cross-linguistic transfer relationship (Cummins, 1978). For example, understanding reading as a process for gaining meaning from text, and that reading comprehension is thinking with and beyond the text, are positive transfer skills. Intentionally teaching students that these concepts and skills have a positive transfer relationship across two languages promotes a deeper understanding and intellectual ability to:

- recognize key ideas and details
- sequence and predict events
- make inferences
- draw conclusions
- discern cause and effect
- recognize propaganda or unsubstantiated claims

Teachers can remind students how the skills they already know can apply to their new language. This facilitates cross-linguistic transfer and promotes metacognitive skills.

Partial Transfer

Partial transfer occurs when there is a similarity of language concept, rule, skill, or task with a slight difference in expected response. In other words, there are elements that transfer, but not completely.

For example, English and Spanish compound words occur when two words combine to make a new word. In both languages, verbs, nouns, and adjectives are used to form compound words. However, while some compound words refer to the same object or concept, they cannot be literally translated.

Spanish	English
lavaplatos	dishwasher
baloncesto	basketball
girasol	sunflower

"Teachers can remind students how the skills they already know can apply to their new language."

Negative Transfer

Negative transfer refers to a linguistic condition where performance on the first task inhibits or detracts from performance on the second, or a new response is expected from a similar stimulus. Negative transfer, sometimes known as interference, occurs when differences between the structure or elements of two languages lead to errors in the learning of the new language. Words that look the same in English and Spanish and are not cognates are an example of negative transfer.

Spanish	English
dime	dime
meaning: "tell me"	meaning: "ten cents"

When negative transfer occurs, the student is naturally applying what they know in their known language to the new language, not always realizing that the structure or specific rules in each language differ. This dissonance can lead to unintentional errors and breakdown in comprehension.

When teachers understand how students apply their known language to the learned language, they can provide effective feedback and explain to students the rules, conditions, and expected response that apply. Intentionally helping students unravel their generalizations from one language to another and be responsive to their approximations as they grow in understanding how the new language works, motivates students and improves their performance (Bialystok, 2007; Howard et al., 2018).

Helping students unravel generalizations from one language to another improves their performance and motivation.

Zero Transfer

Zero transfer is when there is no influence between prior learning and new learning. There are unique aspects in each language, and the differences between the two languages must be taught specifically and separately. Essentially, there is no ability to transfer because of linguistic differences.

Spanish	English
letter **ñ**	apostrophe **s** (**'s**)
Does not exist in English	In Spanish, possession is indicated with a preposition **de**

Once the specific linguistic elements that characterize a language are taught explicitly in said language, teachers simply point out and clarify that those elements do not exist or are not applicable in the same way to the new language.

Research on transfer of language learning has been very consistent in pointing out that the strength of the known knowledge determines the extent of transfer in the new knowledge (Thonis, 1983). Therefore, it is important to consider the relationships between what is already known and new knowledge. In other words, a student's prior knowledge and learning experiences have a considerable influence on future learning. This is why eliciting prior knowledge, reviewing known concepts, and connecting to previous learning are all fundamental lesson-design components.

As powerful and logical as these transfer relationships between two languages are, transfer cannot be assumed to occur without proper teaching, monitoring, and guidance. Teachers facilitate the transfer connections by consciously planning to point out these transfer relationships to students as they become evident.

Pause and Reflect

In your own words, how do explicitly teaching language and literacy universals support cross-linguistic transfer?

What type of transfer is likely the most difficult for learners of a new language to navigate?

Conclusion

Language universals are often considered evidence of innate language abilities and structures common to all humans. Language enables humans to convey abstract and complex ideas, thoughts, and emotions. Whether through shared environmental influences, or a range of sociocultural factors, humans can acquire multiple languages.

Language and literacy universals help us understand the basic functions and structures that underlie all languages. The language subsystems are components of language and literacy across languages and refer to distinct aspects of language. Language subsystems can therefore be used as a framework to organize cross-linguistic transfer instruction.

Explicit cross-linguistic transfer instruction involves intentionally teaching the similarities and differences between languages to support learners as they transfer their existing linguistic knowledge to a new language. Therefore, there are two important considerations to always keep in mind: the strength of the initial or existing knowledge or understanding, and the linguistic relationship between the two languages being learned.

Key Takeaways

Language universals are common rules and characteristics that all languages share.

Literacy universals are the common characteristics of alphabetical written languages.

There are seven language subsystems that can be used as a framework to organize instruction for cross-linguistic transfer.

Two key constructs affect retention and transfer of skills across languages: the strength of the initial knowledge and the variations in the transfer relationships between the languages (positive, partial, negative, zero).

Chapter 3

Designing Instruction Across Languages

"Effective bilingual education programs should leverage cross-linguistic transfer by promoting metalinguistic awareness and explicitly teaching students to make connections between their languages. This can foster a deeper understanding of language structures and enhance both languages."

"Los programas eficaces de educación bilingüe deben aprovechar la transferencia interlingüística fomentando la conciencia metalingüística y enseñando explícitamente a los alumnos a establecer conexiones entre sus idiomas. Esto puede fomentar una comprensión más profunda de las estructuras lingüísticas y mejorar ambas lenguas".

–James Cummins, 1978

Explicit planning and systematic organization of instruction are necessary to teach cross-linguistic transfer efficiently and effectively. Lessons need to reflect appropriate grade-level standards and follow a coherent scope and sequence at each grade and across grade levels.

In this chapter, we will examine the conditions, organization, and strategies that promote cross-linguistic transfer. I will introduce the three instructional contexts for teaching the same cross-linguistic skill set. Central to this framework is the transfer or "bridge" lesson and its instructional sequence.

In This Chapter

Conditions for Cross-Linguistic Transfer

Teaching for transfer in a biliteracy context requires the strategic use of both languages during instruction. Teachers facilitate the purposeful engagement of students as they connect, compare, or contrast the linguistic features of each language. This engagement and negotiation of the two language systems enhances students' metalinguistic and metacognitive skills resulting in biliteracy development.

There are general conditions that promote cross-linguistic transfer.

Condition	Description
Language Similarity	This is when two languages come from the same linguistic family or lineage, for example the romance languages that evolved from Latin such as Spanish, Portuguese, French, or Romanian. Although English is a Germanic language, a significant portion (60 percent) of the English lexicon, particularly academic vocabulary, is derived from Latin.
L1 Proficiency	When learners have a strong foundation in their first language, they are more likely to transfer skills or knowledge from the first language to the second language.
Explicit Instruction	Cross-linguistic transfer is more likely to occur when explicit instruction is provided in one language and concepts are connected, compared, and contrasted to the partner language.
Attitude Toward Languages	When students have a positive, asset-oriented attitude toward language learning and understand the value of biliteracy in their lives, they are motivated to apply known skills to a new language.
Authentic Practice	Cross-linguistic knowledge is activated when learners have opportunities to use their first language as a resource in learning a new language and when they can practice the new language in authentic contexts.

Eleanor Thonis (1983) provided specific considerations when defining transfer of learning as the application of skills, knowledge, and processes learned in one language context to another language. Specifically, she noted that in a biliteracy context transfer of learning is facilitated when there is:

- similarity in the learning condition
- similarity in the learning task
- similarity in the expected student response
- a comprehensible connection between the first and second learning
- a clear understanding of rules or generalizations

Similarity of learning conditions, task, and expected student response imply that skills from one learning activity transfer to another if the critical features of the second activity resemble those of the first. Learners generalize from their experiences and apply what they know to new learning. The strength and understanding of the original learning greatly influence the extent to which successful new learning can occur (Thonis, 1983). In other words, unknown concepts and skills do not transfer to new language learning.

Transfer of skills is facilitated when certain learning conditions are met.

Similarity of Learning Conditions

Valuing both languages equitably means recognizing the importance of each language in the learning process and ensuring that both languages are given equal attention and respect. This includes that students are provided with equal opportunities to learn and use both languages.

Establishing similarity of learning conditions requires parallel structures that maximize making connections between concepts learned in one language pertinent to the other. For example, unit topics, essential questions, and learning objectives are addressed and discussed using strategies such as note-taking, text annotation, and using anchor charts and graphic organizers. When teachers use similar routines, as well as teaching and learning strategies, in each language, students can connect and internalize concepts in each language.

Biliteracy Context	Examples Across Languages
Similarity of Learning Conditions	▪ equitable and parallel standards, assessments, and curriculum-honoring in each language ▪ parallel unit topics and informational texts ▪ authentic literature in each language ▪ parallel use of instructional routines and methodologies as applicable to each language
Similarity of Learning Tasks	▪ grade-level rigor ▪ appropriate and engaging learning activities ▪ systems for differentiation of assignments and tasks ▪ systems for spiral review and interventions
Similarity of the Expected Response	▪ writing rubrics and prompts ▪ accountable talk ▪ engagement and collaboration ▪ establishment of classroom norms
Comprehensible Connections	▪ teaching and learning opportunities where language concepts and constructs are explicitly connected, compared, and contrasted
Clear Understanding of Rules and Generalization	▪ opportunities to review and restate concepts and constructs learned and how they are or are not applicable in each language ▪ ample learning and practice opportunities to demonstrate independence level and mastery in both languages

Similarity of Learning Tasks

Learning tasks refer to specific, engaging activities or collaborative assignments designed to facilitate the acquisition of knowledge or skills. Learning tasks enable students to practice and apply previously taught concepts and skills. In a biliteracy instructional context, there are appropriate grade-level activities in each language that are differentiated to meet students' academic and linguistic needs. There is also a similarity in the types of tasks assigned at various times in each language. For example, in each language students engage in these tasks:

- Read closely and annotate text using similar notation methods.
- Conduct word studies and take spelling tests.
- Prepare and deliver oral presentations.
- Collaborate with peers to complete projects.
- Complete independent assignments for progress monitoring.

When teachers establish a system of learning tasks that is similar in each language, it is easier for the learner to engage actively with understanding regardless of the language of instruction.

Learn More

Howard, E. J., Lindholm-Leary, K., Rogers, D., Olague, N., Medina, J., Kennedy, B., Sugarman, J., & Christian, D. (2018). *Guiding principles for dual language education* (3rd ed.). Center for Applied Linguistics.

Beeman, K., & Urow, C. (2012). *Teaching for biliteracy: Strengthening bridges between languages*. Brookes Publishing.

Similarity of the Expected Response

Valuing both languages means recognizing the importance of each language in the learning and evaluation processes. This includes ensuring that students are provided with equal opportunities to learn, apply, and show what they can do in both languages. Similarity of expected response also includes classroom and engagement norms. Students should be expected to follow similar procedures, routines, and academic behaviors regardless of the language of instruction. For example, in each language context students:

- follow respectful and collegiate norms of behaviors
- understand what is expected in assignments and are accountable for turning in their assignments
- have differentiation and intervention opportunities
- are monitored and evaluated consistently

Establishing similarity of expected responses affirms equity, value, and respect for each language. This can lead to improved academic outcomes and a healthy academic culture across languages.

Establishing norms for expected responses promotes cross-linguistic transfer.

Comprehensible Connections

Making comprehensible connections across languages is fundamental to cross-linguistic transfer. This can be achieved through various strategies and techniques. Making the connections between languages explicitly is best done through direct instruction. (Direct and explicit cross-linguistic instruction lessons will be addressed in the second part of this book.) However, comprehensible connections between languages can also be made in collaborative groups and during student independent work time. Here are some effective approaches that facilitate establishing connections between languages:

Examples of parallel texts

- Use parallel texts to compare text features, vocabulary, and content.*
- Use bilingual dictionaries to look up word meaning.
- Focus on Greek and Latin roots (word study).
- Analyze language patterns and structures.
- Interpret idioms and figurative language.

When making comprehensible connections between languages, teachers explicitly connect concepts and skills taught in one language to the other through direct instruction. They also facilitate ways for students to use reference texts and resources to connect, compare, and contrast one language to the other.

*Parallel texts should be used judiciously—only a section, paragraph, or page of the text is used for the purpose of contrastive analysis during a designated bridging time.

Clear Understanding of Rules and Generalizations

Establishing a clear understanding of the rules and generalizations specific to each language and across languages involves explicit and selective attention to the language feature being addressed. It also involves providing opportunities for active study, practice, and exposure over time. Teachers facilitate clear understanding of the rules and generalizations specific to each language and across languages by:

- direct and explicit teaching of each language rule
- direct and explicit teaching of generalizations across languages
- parallel deconstruction of sentences
- discussing commonalities and exceptions between languages
- providing feedback to students during formative assessment or conferencing

When students engage in reviewing and restating what they learned about each language and have multiple opportunities to show their understanding of how each language works and does not work, they develop metacognitive and metalinguistic awareness that leads to biliteracy.

> “Making comprehensible connections across languages is fundamental to cross-linguistic transfer.”

Organizing Cross-Linguistic Instruction

Beyond establishing the right conditions to promote the transfer of language learning, instruction should also be organized in a particular way that facilitates comparing and contrasting linguistic features. To reap the potential benefits of interdependence, instruction must focus on language and literacy development in both languages, and indeed focus directly on explicit teaching for transfer (August et al., 2002). When cross-linguistic transfer is taught explicitly, students can avail themselves of concepts and skills already known in one language to learn the other.

In the context of explicit skill-transfer instruction, one language becomes the **instructional language** while the **target language** becomes the **content** of the instruction.

The **instructional language** is used to **deliver** the lesson by

- reviewing known concepts and key academic vocabulary,
- explaining the similarities or differences between one language and the other, and
- negotiating meaning.

The **target language** is the **content** of the lesson, and it is used to

- reintroduce the concept and academic vocabulary,
- demonstrate how the selected features are similar or different, and
- engage in collaborative or independent practice.

Teachers use graphic organizers, posters, visuals, color-coding, charts, sentence strips, word cards, and other manipulatives to enhance the teaching and learning experience.

Explicitly Teaching for Cross-Linguistic Transfer

Research affirms that explicit teaching of cross-linguistic transfer in biliteracy contexts enhances students' understanding and control of linguistic resources across languages (Bialystok, 2007; Howard et al., 2018). Instruction in one language builds on concepts learned in the other language. Therefore, by judicious planning, teachers can make clear, purposeful instructional connections across languages so that biliteracy builds over time.

Explicitly and strategically teaching for cross-linguistic transfer

- alleviates students' burden of having to learn a skill or concept in a language they do not yet understand, and
- enables access to rigorous grade-level content.

Key Terms

Instructional Language: This is the language used by the teacher to convey instructions and explanations to the students. It serves as the medium of instruction. For example, if a teacher uses Spanish to make the cross-linguistic connection to English, then Spanish is the instructional language.

Target Language: This is the language that students are learning or acquiring through the instruction. It is the content of the lesson and the focus of language learning process. For example, when a lesson is taught in Spanish during cross-linguistic transfer time and the content of the learning is English, then English is the target language.

The Bridge and Bridging

Transfer of skill instruction demands that we think about when, how, and in what language cross-linguistic transfer is taught. There are three instructional contexts for teaching the same cross-linguistic skill set.

Partner Language Lesson	Transfer Lesson	Partner Language Lesson
Core instruction in Spanish	Spanish-English cross-linguistic lesson	Core instruction in English
Concept introduced, taught, and independently practiced	Concept or skill connected, compared, and contrasted to the other partner language; the cross-linguistic relationship between the languages is explained	Previously taught concept or skill reviewed and practiced

A skill is first taught in one language during core instruction time. Next, the skill is explicitly addressed for cross-linguistic transfer during a designated time. Finally, the same skill is reviewed, practiced, and expanded in the partner language to reinforce understanding and application. This progression provides three opportunities for teaching, learning, and negotiating the same skill or concept, using a coherent sequence and instructional model.

This process is bidirectional. In other words, the cross-linguistic transfer process can begin in either of the partner languages.

> "In the context of explicit skill-transfer instruction, one language becomes the instructional language while the target language becomes the content of the instruction."

The transfer lesson, therefore, is comparable to a bridge that provides the opportunity for consciously and purposefully teaching transfer through standards-based planning. During a transfer lesson, the "bridge time" is when students transfer what they have learned in one language to the other language.

Beeman and Urow (2012, p. 4) define the terms *bridge* and *bridging* as follows:

- The *bridge* is the instructional moment in teaching dual language when teachers bring the two languages together, guiding students to engage in contrastive analysis of the two languages and transfer the academic content they have learned in one language to the other language.
- *Bridging* involves the use of cross-linguistic strategies and leads to the development of metalinguistic awareness.

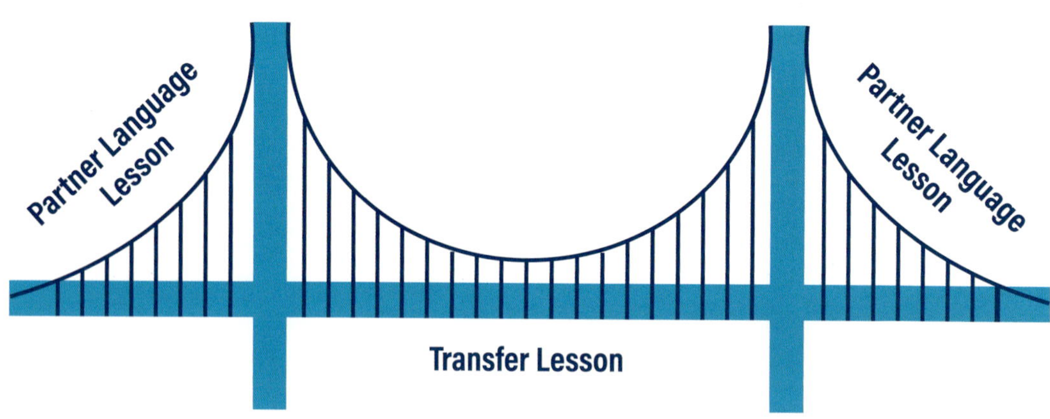

Planning a Standards-Based Transfer Lesson

Planning for cross-linguistic skills transfer involves designing activities and strategies that help students transfer the knowledge and skills gained in the instructional language as they connect to, compare, and contrast with the target language. Cross-linguistic transfer lessons are lessons where teachers model, encourage collaborative practice, and promote metacognitive and metalinguistic understanding.

In the lesson, we identify essential grade-level skill sets and analyze the transference relationship between the two languages. The language of instruction, the language content, and the language of interaction are well defined.

Here is a list of basic steps for planning a cross-linguistic lesson:

1. Determine grade-level standards targets in both languages.
2. Set clear objectives.
3. Recognize the language subsystem.
4. Analyze the transference relationship between the two languages.
5. Plan transfer by designing the lesson sequence.
6. Design teaching and learning activities.
7. Prepare instructional materials.
8. Teach explicitly in the first partner language.
9. Explicitly link language skills from one language to the other.
10. Teach explicitly in the other partner language.
11. Monitor student understanding and assess formatively.

Transfer Lesson Sequence

Explicit teaching of skill transference begins with an overt acknowledgment to students that they already know a skill or concept and that they are ready to learn and apply what they already know in another language. During the transfer lesson, there is a gradual release of language use. The language transfer will connect the language taught to the target language. The table below outlines the scaffolded lesson sequence of a transfer lesson (bridge time), beginning with orientation and ending with independent practice.

Transfer Lesson Sequence	Teacher Actions
Orientation	• Activate prior knowledge. • Make connections between the instructional language and the target language. • State lesson objectives. • Provide comprehensible connections between the partner languages.
Presentation	• Explain, demonstrate, and give examples of the concept and skill strategy. • Point out the similarity or differences in the learning conditions and tasks.
Structured Guided Practice	• Lead students step by step, clarifying concepts and vocabulary and using concrete/visual representations. • Negotiate the rules and conditions applicable to the skill or task (ongoing).
Collaborative Practice	• Encourage collaboration between students. • Elicit metacognitive skills. • Provide corrective feedback as students practice.
Independent Practice	• Ensure that students are working at an appropriate level of L2 language proficiency.

In planning the instructional sequence that ensures transfer from one language skill and concept to another, teachers need to consider the successive approximations or scaffolding needed during independent work at each student's level of language acquisition.

Cross-Linguistic Strategies

Cross-linguistic strategies are most often implemented during the "bridge time" of the transfer lesson. The bridge is a designated time during an instructional sequence or lesson when the focus of instruction is for students to transfer what they have learned in one language to the other language. The instructional focus moves from teaching content, to teaching about how language works in each language. Bridging is also the time when teachers can explicitly teach contrastive analysis, pointing out how the two languages are the same or where there is a linguistic element specific to each language.

During bridging, teachers explicitly teach contrastive analysis, pointing out similarities or differences between the languages.

Strategies by Language Subsystem

There are several strategies teachers can use within each language subsystem. In this way, teachers plan cross-linguistic strategies that promote metalinguistic and metacognitive skills. Part 2 of this book explains how to teach each subsystem in a dual-language setting.

Language Subsystem	Cross-Linguistic Strategies
Phonology	▪ Compare and contrast sounds to discern if they are the same or different in each language. ▪ Analyze prosody and intonation in questions, commands, and statements.
Orthography	▪ Notice letter patterns in each language. ▪ Have students analyze their spelling approximations. ▪ Explicitly point out syllabication and spelling in cognate words.
Morphology	▪ Study academic cognates and false cognates. ▪ Analyze and generate words that share the same Greek and Latin prefixes, roots, and suffixes in both languages. ▪ Generate word derivatives in both languages. ▪ Study word origins and the way their meanings may have changed throughout history.
Semantics	▪ Study and compare word relationships in each language. ▪ Compare and contrast word use, and word nuances, used in the same context for both languages. ▪ Create bilingual dictionaries, pictorial charts, and/or vocabulary graphic organizers to translate key terms.
Grammar and Syntax	▪ Analyze the place of a word or phrase in a sentence. ▪ Deconstruct and translate a phrase or sentence. ▪ Interpret idioms and cultural expressions in each language. ▪ Analyze sentence structures and grammatical constructions in translated sentences.
Pragmatics	▪ Shift language use based on task, purpose, audience, and text type in each language using the same context. ▪ Notice informal and formal language use in each language; for example, greetings, farewells, requests for information, and other interpersonal communication.

Additional Cross-Linguistic Strategies

Another way to make cross-linguistic connections is by conducting contrastive analysis at the word, phrase, sentence, and whole-text levels. This strategy is similar to conducting a close reading from a linguistic perspective using parallel texts, which are paired translated texts explicitly chosen for contrastive analysis. Teacher and students compare text features, academic language, transition words, and text structures as they focus on how language works in each language. Use of parallel text analysis enhances the learners' ability to monitor their own metalinguistic knowledge and confirms their vocabulary and syntactical awareness (Mora & Dorta-Duque de Reyes, in press).

There are other ways to promote cross-linguistic transfer and language connections. These strategies go beyond explicit instruction and encourage a sense of metalinguistic and metacognitive discovery. Here are some examples:

- Read text in one language—discuss and expand ideas in the other.
- Compare and contrast a text read in one language with a text read in another language.
- Compare and contrast cultural language use, such as commercials, jingles, advertisements, newspapers, and news reports.
- Select key academic terms or content-specific terms and translate the term into multiple languages; for example, *photosynthesis* in Spanish, German, Mandarin.
- Read text in one language and use it as a reference or springboard to write about the topic in the other language.

Discourse Strategies

Discourse refers to the sustained use of language in a larger context, beyond phrase or sentence level. It is the way language is used to convey meaning and conduct communication in various social and cultural settings. It is associated with formal and academic language, and it encompasses the organization of ideas in both spoken and written language in light of the relationship between speakers or writers and their audience.

Discourse is the use of language to accomplish specific communication goals, such as persuading, informing, or entertaining. Discourse may be classified as:

- descriptive
- narrative
- expository
- argumentative

Distinct types of oral discourse include:

- conversations
- interviews
- speeches
- storytelling

Teaching discourse strategies involves text analysis and includes noticing language patterns, such as transitions between ideas and sentences. There are many techniques associated with oral and written discourse such as the use of summarization, analogies, arguments and counter arguments, figurative language, and many others.

Discourse techniques in each language are analyzed during cross-linguistic instruction. Language used for expressing agreement, disagreement, clarification, and negotiation are compared and practiced.

In the context of biliteracy, understanding discourse is crucial for effective and proficient communication in each language. Analyzing and understanding discourse provides insights into power dynamics, social practices, and cultural norms embedded in language.

Translation and Interpretation

Translation and interpretation skills are highly valued commodities. Oftentimes our students become translators at an early age. They negotiate meaning for their parents, relatives, and friends in multiple environments. Proficient translation skills require an excellent command of two or more languages and an extensive cultural knowledge of each.

Strategies that engage students in translation beyond the word level are:

- translating sayings, quotes, and short sentences
- role-playing situations where translation or interpretation is needed
- interpreting idioms and cultural expressions

Caveat

A Note About Concurrent Translation

Explaining a concept by constantly and concurrently translating from one language to another is an ineffective way for teaching students a new language. Instead, students should be challenged to apply the knowledge they already possess in one language to the other, through a contrastive analysis of the two languages.

When teaching a cross-linguistic lesson, the teacher uses one language as the instructional language. The target language becomes the content of the lesson. In other words, one language is used to talk about or teach how another language works.

The explicit teaching of skill transference increases students' metalinguistic awareness and promotes high levels of biliteracy.

Translanguaging

Over the past couple of decades, more has been learned about how bilinguals process their two languages. More recently, research has shown that bilinguals activate both languages in parallel when they process or produce language (Kroll & Bialystock, 2013).

Translanguaging is "an act performed by bilinguals of accessing different linguistic features or various modes of what are described as autonomous languages, in order to maximize communicative potential" (García et al., 2017, pp. v-xix). Translanguaging is a dynamic and creative process that enables multilingual students to draw on their linguistic resources to construct meaning and connect to others. In other words, translanguaging is a way that bilingual students use their languages to communicate, negotiate, and access meaning.

In *Guiding Principles for Dual Language Education* (Howard et al., 2018), four purposes for translanguaging are defined:

1. Provide support for students to engage and comprehend academic content.
2. Give students opportunities to engage in language practice while reading academic content.
3. Provide a space for students to further develop their bilingualism.
4. Promote the socio-emotional development of students, especially their bilingual identities.

Translanguaging supports students' academic and personal growth by validating their linguistic identities and providing more inclusive and effective learning experiences. It is considered an equity, access, and justice issue because it addresses systemic inequities in education, promoting a more inclusive and just learning environment for all students.

Example

During collaborative work, students use all their language resources to negotiate meaning when they use translanguaging. They seamlessly blend and switch between languages as they communicate to express their thoughts and intentions.

La teacher said that we had to hacer un mapa de nuestro state.

We are going to need paper y el libro de Social Studies.

I will get el mío. Lo tengo ahí on my desk.

Get el de español también, Okay?

Aquí están los dos. What did teacher just say?

La maestra dijo que el state capital needs to have una estrella para indicar que es important o algo así.

When finished, students present their state poster as they describe the state flag, capital, geographical characteristics, and other interesting facts using only or mostly the designated language of the class.

Pause and Reflect

What two strategies from this chapter would you like to implement or enhance in your instruction?

Why is concurrent translation ineffective for teaching students a new language, and what should be encouraged instead?

According to the translanguaging perspective, emergent bilinguals use all their cognitive and linguistic resources during interactions, such that the content on which they draw may be distributed across languages (Escamilla & Hopewell, 2019). Instructionally, this perspective means there is not a strict separation of languages, but there can be more fluid use of both languages strategically in the same lesson (Lewis et al., 2012).

Conclusion

Teaching for transfer in a biliteracy context requires the strategic use of both languages during instruction. This entails purposeful planning, meticulous design, effective organization, and thoughtful discourse. It is essential to understand that cross-linguistic transfer does not occur spontaneously without guidance from teachers. Teachers promote cross-linguistic transfer by consciously planning and explicitly pointing out the transfer relationships that exist and the learning opportunities embedded in each of the instructional components.

Key Takeaways

Cross-linguistic transfer necessitates planning and organizing instruction explicitly and systematically.

In a biliteracy teaching context, there are various conditions that help promote cross-linguistic transfer.

The language subsystems can act as a guide for strategically planning cross-linguistic instruction.

Chapter 4

Assessment in a Biliteracy Context

"Bilingual means TWO: Assessment for biliteracy requires a positive schema around how two languages interact. Assessment must combine concepts known in the first language with concepts being learned in the second language."

"Bilingüe significa DOS: La evaluación de la alfabetización bilingüe requiere un esquema positivo en torno a la interacción de dos idiomas. La evaluación debe combinar conceptos conocidos en la primera lengua con conceptos que se están aprendiendo en la segunda".

–Kathy Escamilla, 2000

In a biliteracy context, assessments must consider how students' knowledge of one language affects their ability to learn or use another language. This kind of assessment monitors students' progress toward becoming biliterate. More specifically, cross-linguistic assessment involves comparing a student's performance in one language to their performance in another. This comparison provides valuable insight into how each individual student is transferring skills learned in one language to the other.

Biliterate assessment plans are essential to programs that desire a biliteracy outcome. This chapter addresses how to collect and analyze data effectively in dual-language settings.

In This Chapter

Assessment for Biliteracy

Collecting Assessment Data

Interpreting and Analyzing Assessment Data

Assessment for Biliteracy

Assessments in dual-language programs need to be designed with the same rigor, standards, and principles in both languages. Accordingly, assessments in dual-language programs require a positive schema around how the two languages interact. Assessment in the context of biliteracy includes the correlation and analysis of assessment results for concepts known in the first language and concepts being learned in the second language (Escamilla, 2000; Grosjean, 1989).

Assessment in the context of biliteracy

- supports the accountability process by consistently conducting equitable assessments in the two languages of the program,
- considers the student's simultaneous or sequential acquisition of biliteracy,
- uses data purposefully to monitor and ensure student progress in dual-language development, and
- takes into account the influences and interactions of both languages.

“Assessments in dual-language programs need to be designed with the same rigor, standards, and principles in both languages.”

The *Guiding Principles for Dual Language Education* (Howard et al., 2018) state that research on effective schools, including effective bilingual and dual-language programs, emphasizes the key role of assessment and accountability. A substantial number of studies have converged on the significance of using student achievement data to shape and/or monitor instruction and the instructional program in bilingual settings (Corallo & McDonald, 2002; Linquanti & Hakuta, 2012; Minicucci et al., 1995; National Research Council and Institute of Medicine, 1997; Reyes et al., 1999; Slavin & Calderón, 2001). Effective dual-language programs use multiple valid and reliable measures in both languages to:

Assessment data informs teaching decisions.

- assess students' progress toward meeting bilingual and biliteracy goals along with the curricular and content-related goals
- identify and address issues of curriculum, assessment, and instructional alignment (Corallo & McDonald, 2002; Escamilla, 2000)
- evaluate program effectiveness
- communicate assessment results with the larger community

Solano-Flores and Trumbull (2003) argue that new research and assessment practices need to be developed that include providing the same items in English and the native language, and that this will lead to more valid and reliable assessment outcomes. Effective schools use assessment measures that are aligned with the school's vision and goals, and with appropriate curriculum and related standards (Lindholm-Leary & Molina, 2000; Montecel & Cortez, 2002).

Learn More

Escamilla, K., Hopewell, S., Butvilofsky, S., Sparrow, W., & Soltero-González, L. (2014). *Biliteracy from the start: Literacy squared in action* (Reprint ed.). Brookes Publishing.

Howard, E. J., Lindholm-Leary, K., Rogers, D., Olague, N., Medina, J., Kennedy, B., Sugarman, J., & Christian, D. (2018). *Guiding principles for dual language education* (3rd ed.). Center for Applied Linguistics.

A Holistic and Additive Approach to Assessment

The following are essential to establishing a holistic biliteracy approach to assessment (Escamilla et al., 2014). Keep these in mind as you plan and develop assessments in a biliteracy classroom:

- Languages are viewed as mutually reinforcing.
- Literacy assessments are administered separately but analyzed in both languages concurrently for cross-linguistic comparison and to document students' biliteracy trajectories.
- Literacy assessment instruments are authentic, considering features of language organization and discourse styles unique to each language.
- Students are expected to show different strengths in the performance of tasks in different languages.
- Bilingual strategies such as code-switching, lexical borrowing, and bidirectional transfer are regarded as part of the process of learning to read and write in two languages.

Collecting Assessment Data

Collecting assessment data in a dual-language classroom setting is essential. Data provides evidence of the progress students are making in both languages. It may also reveal where students need additional practice or support. There are different types of data a teacher can collect. Both quantitative data (scores, grades) and qualitative data (portfolios, observation notes, etc.) provide valuable insight into student progress. When collecting all types of data, it is important to consider multiple sources to make informed instructional decisions.

Key Terms

Valid and Reliable Measures: Assessments that consistently and accurately measure learning.

Holistic Biliteracy Approach: Taking both languages into account, including how the languages interact in teaching and assessment.

Data Triangulation: Using a variety of data from at least three different sources to increase the validity and reliability of the results.

Data Triangulation

Data triangulation is a process of using multiple sources of information or assessment methods to gather a more comprehensive understanding of students' learning, performance or learning modalities. Triangulation involves collecting data from different sources, such as teachers, parents, students, or from various types of student work, including portfolios, observations, and interviews. Compiling data from multiple sources helps teachers gain a comprehensive understanding of students' strengths and learning preferences, which can inform instruction and support student learning as well as promote academic achievement and personal growth. Triangulation helps reduce the biases and limitations that arise from relying on a single language or source of data to monitor, analyze, and evaluate student growth.

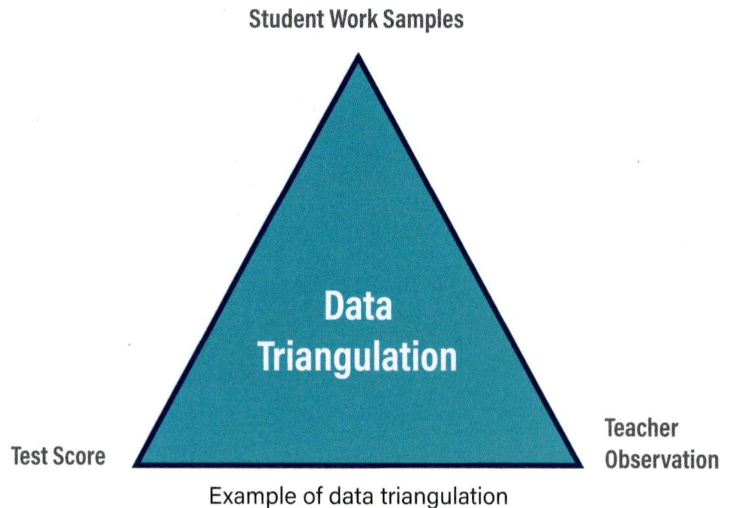

Example of data triangulation

Biliteracy Portfolios

Use biliteracy portfolios to promote agency.

One way to triangulate data is to create biliteracy portfolios. Biliteracy portfolios are collections of student work samples and artifacts that showcase the learning growth and achievements of students who are developing proficiency in two or more languages. Biliteracy portfolios are a powerful tool that serve several purposes—including assessment, communication, and planning—but also give students ownership and a sense of agency over their work. They can be used in a variety of educational contexts including dual-language programs, immersion programs, and English-language development programs. Bilingual student portfolios may include:

- work samples in both languages to demonstrate students' proficiency (e.g., written work, video recording of presentations, student-chosen class assignments or artifacts)
- proficiency assessments in each language to provide evidence of progress over time for each language domain
- cultural artifacts such as biographical accounts, photos, videos, posters, and artwork that show students' understanding of their culture and the culture of others
- written reflections in both languages that indicate metalinguistic awareness and student agency
- portfolio reviews where students present their work and get feedback from their peers, teachers, and parents

Biliteracy portfolios promote bilingualism and multiculturalism. They show academic success and foster students' ability to take charge of their own learning. Learning is enhanced when assessment is owned and understood by the learners themselves. Biliteracy portfolios help students develop agency as they reflect on their learning process, language acquisition, challenges, and outcomes.

Assessing Fluency

One important area of language instruction in a dual-language classroom is fluency. Fluency is the ability to read a text accurately, at an appropriate pace, and with prosody. Fluent readers can read with automaticity. This means they can read without devoting attention to decoding each part of a word. They also group words seamlessly into phrases to gain meaning from what they read. Fluent readers read aloud effortlessly and with expression.

Fluency is important because it relates to word recognition and comprehension. Since fluent readers do not have to concentrate on decoding the words, they can focus their attention on the meaning of the text. They can make connections between the ideas in the text, and they can draw upon their prior knowledge as they read to infer deeper meaning. These connections are essential in cross-linguistic instruction. Fluency allows the brain to process text more effortlessly, freeing cognitive resources for comprehension and transfer between languages. A fluent reader can better focus on understanding similarities and differences in linguistic structures, vocabulary, and meaning across languages. Fluency often comes with a solid grasp of a language's syntax and grammar. When learning another language, these underlying linguistic patterns can be applied or adapted, speeding up the acquisition process.

In both English and Spanish, repeated and monitored oral reading improves reading fluency and overall fluency comprehension. You can help your students become more fluent readers by:

- providing them with models of fluent reading in both languages
- listening to and guiding them as they read and reread passages
- practicing choral reading (the whole class reads aloud simultaneously or as an echo)
- assigning partner reading (students read aloud to a partner)
- employing reader's theater (some students rehearse and perform a dialogue-rich script before an audience)

To master fluency, students must first understand what fluent reading sounds like. From there, they will be more likely to transfer those experiences into their own reading. To cultivate fluency in two languages, students require abundant opportunities to engage with read-alouds, where they can hear the rhythm, tone, and pacing that define fluent reading in each language. Regular exposure to these read-alouds is essential for internalizing the flow of language and to building the ability to read confidently and effortlessly in both languages.

In both English and Spanish, there are similar teaching methodologies and learning tasks associated with fluency: reading aloud, demonstrating prosody, incorporating repeated readings, echo reading, chiming, and paired reading. Instructors explicitly teach students that reading fluently means reading with purpose, at the right pace, using their voice to express meaning—including pausing and phrasing—and paying careful attention to punctuation.

Caveat

An Important Caveat for Fluency Assessment

Fluency rates for English should not be applied to Spanish reading. English fluency rates average 27 words per minute more than Spanish rates. A "total words per minute" scoring guide normed with English readers reading English passages is not a valid measure for Spanish reading fluency (Ramírez & Larrea-García, 2015).

Benchmark Education has heeded this recommendation, concurring with both bilingual education practitioners and researchers, to establish recommended fluency rates for Spanish readers. These rates align to studies from countries with native Spanish speakers.

Below are the recommended English and Spanish fluency rates for Foundational Skills Assessments targets for 2020–2021. They are used in *Benchmark Advance/Adelante* and are included here for your consideration.

English Fluency Reading Rate Goals (words per minute)

Grade	Beginning of Year	Middle of Year	End of Year
1	NA *	29	60
2	50	84	100
3	83	97	112
4	94	120	133
5	121	133	146
6	132	145	146

* not required until middle of Grade 1; 50th percentile ranking recommended (Hasbrouck & Tindal, 2017)

Spanish Fluency Reading Rate Goals (words per minute)

Grade	Beginning of Year	Middle of Year	End of Year
1	NA *	23	47
2	32	52	73
3	65	84	93
4	76	94	112
5	103	116	129
6	114	121	129

* not required until middle of Grade 1; suggested goals adapted from Ramírez & Larrea-García (2015)

Interpreting and Analyzing Assessment Data

After assessment data is collected, it needs to be interpreted and analyzed in a systematic way. The accurate interpretation of assessment outcomes involves understanding research and practices in dual-language education and establishing appropriate expectations for students who are taught and tested in two languages. In addition, because of the significance of assessment for both accountability and program evaluation purposes, it is important to establish a data management system that monitors student progress over time.

Key Terms

Mean: The sum of all the numbers in a data set divided by the number of values in the set.

Median: The middle value in a data set that has been ordered from least to greatest.

Mode: The number that appears most often in a data set.

Analysis of quantitative data involves the interpretation of descriptive statistics like measures of central tendency (mean, median, mode). These statistics may inform how a student performs in comparison to benchmarks or norms.

In contrast, qualitative data interpretation involves a search for repeated patterns in student work, behaviors, and knowledge. Teachers can observe students, make notes, and use tasks such as written responses to determine student progress. This kind of descriptive analysis also informs instructional decisions.

Interpretation and analysis of assessment data is critical in a dual-language setting because it tells us how students are progressing in both languages. As such, it is important for educators to participate in continued professional development that is focused on assessment and the interpretation of data (Levine & Lezotte, 2003; Montecel & Cortez, 2002).

Use a variety of assessments, so students have many opportunities to demonstrate their knowledge.

Pause and Reflect

In your own words, what are two important things to remember when assessing students for biliteracy?

Why should English fluency rates not be applied to Spanish reading?

Conclusion

Assessment is a systematic process of collecting, analyzing, and using information about students' knowledge and skills. It is not a separate activity but an integral part of the teaching and learning process. Assessment for biliteracy demands that we establish an equitable system for monitoring student language and content growth across time. Therefore, dual-language educators must collaboratively design a well-articulated biliteracy assessment plan that not only analyzes student learning in each language but also considers how the languages interact. Biliteracy portfolios are an effective tool for ensuring that multiple sources of data are collected. They also promote student agency and ownership of learning. Portfolios celebrate achievement toward biliteracy. In addition, fluency is a key area of language that needs to be assessed in cross-linguistic instruction. Data should be interpreted and analyzed to inform instructional decisions.

Key Takeaways

Assessments in dual-language programs are designed with the same rigor, standards, and principles in both languages.

Assessment in the context of biliteracy includes the correlation and analysis of assessment results for concepts known in the first language and concepts being learned in the second language.

Fluency rates for English should not be applied to Spanish reading. Authentic Spanish fluency rates should be used instead.

Biliteracy portfolios are an authentic and effective way to demonstrate students' progress toward biliteracy.

Subsistemas del lenguaje

Part 2

Language Subsystems

Part 2 demonstrates the use of the language subsystems as an organizational framework to plan cross-linguistic transfer lessons. An understanding of these systems is imperative for effective cross-linguistic instruction because they provide a way to study the various components of language explicitly across languages. Cross-linguistic connections and comparisons between English and Spanish are described for each subsystem. Cross-linguistic transfer lessons are presented across K–5 settings in the "In Action" section of each chapter.

Chapter 5

Phonology

"They say you can do phonemic awareness instruction in the dark, but should you?"

"Dicen que se puede aprender la conciencia fonémica en la oscuridad, pero ¿deberíamos hacerlo así"?

–Nathan Clemens et al., 2021

In this chapter, we look at phonology and instructional sequences that facilitate students' understanding of how sounds are an essential component of language. The role of phonological awareness and the elements that contribute to the musicality of language in cross-linguistic instruction are explained.

An integral piece of this chapter (and the ones that follow) are the "In Action" lesson sequences. This first one focuses on teaching phonology in a dual-language setting. These sample lessons show what teaching for cross-linguistic instruction looks like across both English and Spanish.

In This Chapter

Phonology: The Musicality of Language

Phonology is the study of the sound system of a language. Every world language has a unique sound system, and phonological similarities and differences exist across languages. Phonology involves the study of various aspects of speech sounds, including the perception, production, and interpretation of sounds. It also relates to the musicality and patterns of sounds in a language, or prosody, and how these patterns are used to convey meaning.

The musicality of a language refers to the rhythm, intonation, and overall auditory qualities that give that language a distinct sound pattern. Just as melodies and rhythms create the unique character of a song or musical piece, languages also have their own patterns of sounds that contribute to their distinctive characteristics. Musical notes can be compared to the sounds of language (Ferreiro, 2002).

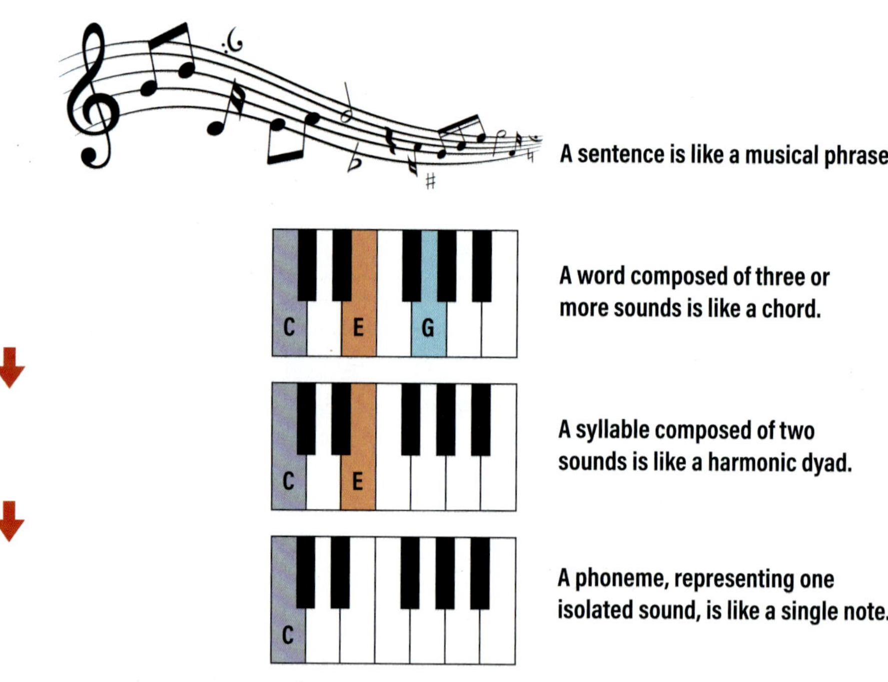

Many features of a language affect the musicality of the language. Here are a few:

- **Phonology and Phonetics:** the specific sounds a language uses and the way they are produced and pronounced
- **Rhythm:** the natural flow and pacing of speech created by the arrangement of stressed and unstressed syllables
- **Intonation:** the rise and fall in pitch to convey meanings, emotions, and nuances such as the rising intonation at the end of a sentence to indicate a question
- **Pitch:** some languages have high pitch variations, while others are more monotone
- **Cadence:** the sequence and flow of words in a language, including the stop and go between words, phrases, and sentences
- **Syllable Structure:** the complexity and variety of syllables that impact the rhythmic and melodic qualities of a language; some languages are multisyllabic by nature, while others have complex syllable structures that lead to intricate sound patterns

The musicality of language is also influenced by culture, which is embedded in the language. Some cultures value a more expressive intonation than others, influencing distinct patterns of speech and communication.

All these elements of musicality work together and play an essential role in understanding and conveying meaning in a language. They represent the linguistic, artistic, and cultural intersection of language and human expression.

Musicality in Poetry

We hear the musicality of language in natural everyday expressions. In particular, the musicality of language is heard in poetry. Dr. Alma Flor Ada and F. Isabel Campoy (2003) remind us that the affinity children have for poetry and its memorable language-rich quality gives poetry great instructional power. Through its rhyme and rhythm, music and magic, imagery and inspiration, children can delight in language.

In any language, the predictable rhythm and rhyme of poems immerse students in the musicality of language, which is fundamental to promoting phonological awareness.

Through poetry, we can also celebrate friendship, relationships, and caring for others as we are exposed to the musicality of languages in Spanish and English. Below is one example.

A de amigos	**Un en un**
A de amigos y alegría, de amiguito y de amiguita. A de abrazos para abuelita.	Un ratón en un botón Un gato en un zapato Una gallina en una tina Un mago en un lago y una nena con una ballena.

Spanish Literacy: Strategies for Young Learners
(Alma Flor Ada & F. Isabel Campoy, 2010)

We can enjoy whimsical and playful rhymes and rhythm as we foster phonological awareness.

Make New Friends	**One, Two, Buckle My Shoe**
Make new friends, But keep the old, One is silver, and the other gold.	One, two: buckle my shoe. Three, four: shut the door. Five, six: pick up sticks. Seven, eight: lay them straight.

(Public domain)

Phonological awareness, poetry, and cross-linguistic transfer are interconnected concepts that relate to language acquisition and development. Phonological awareness refers to the ability to manipulate sounds in language and poetry emphasizes the rhythms, rhymes, and sounds in a language. Phonemic awareness, a subcategory of phonological awareness, relates specifically to the identification of phonemes in a language. By recognizing the musical elements in one language, students can in turn appreciate and learn to recognize the musicality in another language. In addition, understanding the relationship between the structure of two languages and the key elements of poetry, students can enjoy biliteracy and transcend linguistic boundaries.

Dr. Alma Flor Ada (2016) models bilingual poetry in these stanzas from two of her most beloved poems.

Somos amigas	**Bilingüe**
Yo hablo español. Tú hablas inglés. Yo digo ¡sí! Tú dices ¡yes!	Porque soy bilingüe, puedo leer libros y *books.* Tengo amigos y *friends.* Disfruto canciones y *songs,* juegos y *games* y me divierto el doble.

Todo es Canción: Antología Poética (Alma Flor Ada, 2016)

Caveat

A key contrast between Spanish and English literacy instruction is the use of onset-rime structures. Identifying onset and rime is a way to segment words.

Onset is defined as the initial part of the word that precedes the vowel. Rime is the vowel and consonants that follow in the word.

In English, rimes are an effective practice because they form the basis for recognizing sound chunks and patterns, primarily in single-syllable words, facilitating word recognition and patterns in word families. On the other hand, in Spanish it is the phonological awareness of the syllable and syllabic structure that facilitates orthographic patterns and word recognition. Spanish is a syllabic language with a regular and well-defined syllabic structure, which is the most important unit of phonological awareness in the Spanish language (Ferreiro, 2002).

Onset and Rime

c	at
b	at
m	at
r	at

Onset and rime is a great practice for English because of the large number of one-syllable words with short-vowel phonemes and predictable spelling patterns.

Syllabic Decoding

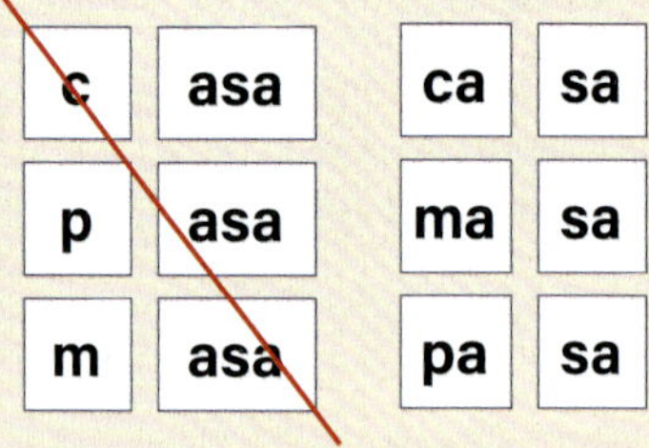

Onset and rime as a segmentation practice is **not** recommended for Spanish because it disrupts the syllabic patterns that are a prominent feature of Spanish phonology.

Phonology and Biliteracy

In the linguistic field of phonology, sounds are analyzed and categorized based on their distinctive features, which are the smallest units of sound that differentiate meaning in a language. For example, adding the /s/ sound to a noun in English often makes it plural, essentially changing the meaning of the word.

In teaching and learning, phonology also relates to the development of phonemic awareness. Phonemic awareness is a metalinguistic skill where students become aware that languages are made up of sounds. As they develop phonemic awareness, students notice, think about, and work with the sounds in words. Before children learn to read print, they need to become aware of the sounds and meanings of words.

Students must understand that words are made up of speech sounds or phonemes. In other words, they need to understand that the sounds of a spoken language work together to make words. Since a minor phonemic change can significantly alter the meaning of a word, students must learn to recognize these differences. Here are some examples of how a change in a single sound can also change the meaning of the word.

Spanish
***c**asa* ***m**asa*
*niñ**a*** *niñ**o***
*pal**e**ta* *pal**i**ta*

English
cat **m**at
boy boy**s**
h**a**t h**o**t

Learn More

Ada, A. F., & Campoy, F. I. (2010) *Spanish literacy: Strategies for young learners*. Frog Street Press.

Ada, A. F., & Campoy, F. I. (2003). *Esta linda la mar*. Santillana USA.

Spanish Phonology

In Spanish phonology, syllables are often considered more important than phonemes for several reasons.

- **Open Syllable Structure:** Spanish has a predominantly open syllable structure, which means that most syllables end with a vowel sound. Spanish syllables follow a relatively consistent pattern of vowel-consonant combinations, which contributes to its phonological structure. In Spanish, the vowel is the nucleus of the syllable.
- **Stress Patterns:** Syllables play a key role in determining stress patterns within words.
- **Word Division:** Knowing where to divide words into syllables is essential for correct spelling and pronunciation. In Spanish, words are divided into syllables that affect accentuation and the placement of accent marks.
- **Verb Conjugation:** Spanish verbs are conjugated by adding suffixes to the verb stem. The syllable-based nature of the language influences how these suffixes are added, contributing to the regularity of verb conjugation patterns.
- **Pronunciation:** The prevalence of open syllables and the relatively straightforward pronunciation of Spanish phonemes contribute to the overall phonetic clarity and ease of pronunciation.

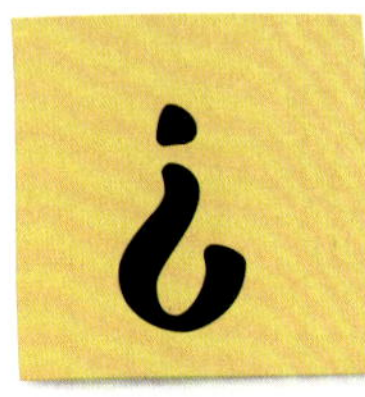

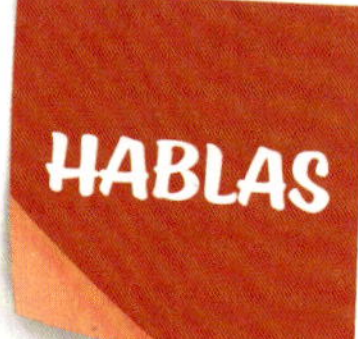

English Phonology

In English, on the other hand, individual phonemes are crucial. There are several reasons why phonemes are so important.

- **Meaning Differentiation:** English has many minimal pairs—pairs of words that differ in only one phoneme, such as *ship* and *sheep* or *pen* and *pan*. The ability to distinguish between the phonemes allows speakers to convey precise meanings. Without the ability to distinguish between the minimal-pair phonemes, words would sound the same.
- **Orthography and Spelling:** Isolating phonemes helps learners grasp how sounds are represented by a variety of written symbols (letters and letter patterns).
- **Complex and Irregular Spelling Patterns:** Recognizing phonemes and how they are represented by various letters and letter patterns is essential to learning to read and write in English.
- **Phonotactics:** The English language has its own set of phonotactics—the permissible ways or patterns in which phonemes can or cannot be combined. For example, English allows consonant clusters at the beginning of words such as *split* and at the end of words such as *branch*. These patterns are complex and are an integral aspect of language processing.

Cross-Linguistic Connections

For all language learners, phonological awareness is an essential skill because it influences the ability to understand spoken language and to produce and pronounce the sounds of a language. A learner's native language may influence the way they perceive and produce sounds in a second language. Therefore, understanding the phonological patterns of a language and how sounds convey meaning helps language learners acquire, understand, and communicate in that language.

Phonological awareness can be explicitly taught. Effective phonological awareness instruction teaches children to notice, think about, and work with (manipulate) sounds in spoken language. In addition to counting, sorting, matching, and calling out syllables and phonemes, teachers use oral activities to build phonological awareness. The tables that follow provide strategies for teaching phonological awareness at the sentence, word, syllable, and phoneme levels.

“For all language learners, phonological awareness is an essential skill because it influences the ability to understand spoken language and to produce and pronounce the sounds of a language.”

Sentence/Phrase Level

Discerning word boundaries or junctures in a sentence is crucial for language learners as they are ascertaining meaning as well as developing fluency and prosody in each language. The strategies shown here support teaching sentence-level or phrase-level phonological awareness in both English and Spanish.

Strategy	Teacher Action(s)	English	Spanish
Poems and Rhymes **Songs and Chanting**	Read a brief poems with rhymes; sing songs and chants with rhythm and movement.	Row, row, row your boat Gently down the stream Merrily, merrily, merrily, merrily Life is but a dream.	Los pollitos dicen, pío, pío, pío, cuando tienen hambre, cuando tienen frío.
Chiming In	Choral read and omit a key phrase, prompting students to chime in the missing phrase.	Mary had a little _____.	Naranja dulce, limón _____.
Alliteration	Share sentences that have 2 or 3 words with the same initial sound or series of sounds.	**L**eo the **l**ion **l**iked to **l**augh.	**Rá**pido co**rr**en los ca**rr**os del fe**rro**ca**rr**il.
Identify the Number of Words in a Sentence	Invite students to repeat and count the words in a short (3–4 word) sentence. Signal each word with a finger or a clap.	We are happy! (1) (2) (3)	¡Todos estamos felices! (1) (2) (3)

Word Level

Word-level analysis helps language learners understand the meaning of words and prepares them to recognize elements within the word. It helps multilingual learners tune in to the sounds features of a specific language.

Strategy	Teacher Action(s)	English	Spanish
Rhyming	Provide rhyming word pairs and encourage students to recognize or generate their own rhyming words.	cat - bat	casa - masa
Odd One Out	Present a group of words and ask students to identify the word that does not rhyme.	cake make *shoe*	carro barro *mesa*
Matching/Pairing Illustrations	Ask students to match rhyming pairs.	hen - pen	pato - gato

Syllable Level

Understanding syllabication is a fundamental skill in both Spanish and English and it begins with phonological awareness. Syllables are units of sounds within a word. Spanish is a multisyllabic language, meaning that most words have two or more syllables. The syllable is used for a phonetic approach to literacy in Spanish. All multisyllabic words have one syllable marked for primary stress. This is important for pronunciation. English is mostly a monosyllabic language where individual phonemes are isolated and recognized. In both Spanish and English, most syllables must contain a vowel.

Strategy	Teacher Action(s)	English	Spanish
Syllable Clapping	Clap as each syllable in a word is segmented.	*mu*-sic	*mú*-si-ca
Syllable Counting	Count each syllable in a word.	to-ma-to (1)-(2)-(3)	to-ma-te (1)-(2)-(3)
Stomp and Clap	Stomp and clap at the same time to mark the syllable with the primary stress.	te - le - phone *	te - lé - fo - no *
Combine Syllables	Pronounce syllables slowly and have learners blend them together to form a word.	*Let's blend the syllables together to make a word: mo - ther. What's the word? Mother.*	*Vamos a combinar estas sílabas para formar una palabra: za - pa - to ¿Qué palabra es? Zapato.*
Segment Syllables	Provide a word and ask learners to break it down by its syllables.	*The word is basketball. Sound out the syllables. bas - ket - ball.*	*La palabra es mariposa. Divídanla en sílabas. ma - ri - po - sa.*
Syllabic Isolation	Present a word and ask students to identify and isolate a specific syllable.	*What is the first syllable in umbrella? /um/. What is the last syllable in umbrella? /la/.*	*¿Cuál es la primera sílaba en la palabra masa? /ma/. ¿Cuál es la última sílaba en la palabra masa? /sa/.*
Adding Syllables	Provide a word and ask students to add a syllable to make a new word.	*The word is cow. Add /boy/ at the end. The new word is cowboy.*	*La palabra es gira, añade la sílaba /sol/ al final. La palabra nueva es: gisarol.*
Deleting Syllables	Provide a word and ask students to delete a syllable to make a new word.	*The word is toothbrush. Take away /brush/ at the end. The new word is tooth.*	*La palabra es pelota, quítale la sílaba final /ta/. La palabra nueva es: pelo.*
Substituting Syllables	Provide a word and ask students to change one syllable for another to make a new word.	*The word is blueberry. Now change /blue/ to /straw/. The new word is strawberry.*	*La palabra es pato. Cambia la sílaba /pa/ por /ga/. La palabra nueva es: gato.*

Phoneme Level

Phonemic awareness is crucial in the development of language and literacy in English and Spanish. The ability to recognize and manipulate sounds in each language enhances the ability of students to produce and distinguish sounds for both. This chart shows the various activities that promote phonemic awareness. Notice that in Spanish, phonemic awareness includes syllabic awareness. Syllabic awareness in Spanish is important because of the multisyllabic structure of the Spanish language and its close ties to accentuation. Strong syllabic awareness helps learners know where to place stress within words.

Strategy	Teacher Action(s)	English	Spanish
Isolating Phonemes	Present a word and ask students to identify and isolate a specific phoneme.	*What is the first sound in sun? /s/. What is the last sound in sun? /n/.*	*¿Cuál es el primer sonido en sol? /s/. ¿Cuál es el último sonido en sol? /l/.*
Blending Phonemes	Pronounce individual phonemes slowly and have learners blend them together to form a word.	*Listen to these sounds then blend them: /c/ /a/ /t/. What is the word? Cat.*	*Escuchen estos sonidos y combínenlos: /s/ /a/ /l/. ¿Qué palabra es? Sal.*
Segmenting Phonemes	Provide a CVC word and ask learners to break it down into individual phonemes.	*What sounds do you hear in the word dog? /d/ – /o/ – /g/.*	*¿Qué sonidos escuchas en la palabra mar? /m/ – /a/ – /r/.*
Segmenting Syllables	Provide a CV-CV word and ask learners to break it down into its syllables.	This is not applicable in early literacy development.	*Escuchen esta palabra: casa Separen la palabra casa por sus sílabas. /ca/ – /sa/.*
Blending Syllables	Present a consonant and ask students to blend its sound with a vowel to form a CV word or syllable.	This is not applicable in early literacy development.	*Escuchen estos sonidos y combínenlos. /m/ /i/. ¿Qué palabra es? Mi.*

In addition to isolating, blending, and segmenting, phonemes can be added, deleted, and substituted. Note that syllable substitution is unique to Spanish in early literacy development.

Strategy	Teacher Action(s)	English	Spanish
Addition	Provide a word and ask learners to add a sound.	*The word is boy.* *Add the /s/ sound at the end.* *The new word is boys.*	*La palabra es niño.* *Añade el sonido /s/ al final.* *La palabra nueva es: niños.*
Deletion	Provide a word and ask learners to add a sound.	*The word is cat.* *Take away the first sound.* */c/ at.* *What is the new word? at.*	*La palabra es niñas.* *Quita la /s/ al final.* *¿Qué palabra queda? Niña.*
Substitution	Provide a word and ask learners to exchange one phoneme for another.	*The word is pat.* *Change the /a/ to an /e/.* *What is the new word? Pet.*	*La palabra es pala.* *Cambia la /a/ final y pon una /o/.* *¿Qué palabra formaste? Palo.*
Syllable Substitution	Provide a CV-CV word and ask learners to exchange one syllable for another.	This is not applicable in early literacy development.	*La palabra es masa.* *Cambia la sílaba /ma/ y pon /me/.* *¿Qué palabra formaste? Mesa.*

In a dual-language context, phonological routines and word play like those above are strategies that promote cross-linguistic transfer by similarity of learning condition. Similarity of learning condition refers to the degree of resemblance or likeness between methodologies used in one language environment and the other. When the instructional methods and materials in one language context are similar to those in the other language context, then the transfer of skills and knowledge from one language to another is facilitated.

Elkonin Boxes

Elkonin Boxes are a visual and tactile tool that help all students develop phonemic awareness skills. They provide a visual representation of phonemes and help students understand that words are made up of individual sounds.

Elkonin boxes are named after the Russian psychologist, Dr. David Elkonin, who worked in collaboration with Lev Vygotsky. Together, they have had a significant influence on our understanding of how children learn and develop literacy and language.

Elkonin boxes are a series of empty squares arranged in a row. The number of boxes corresponds to the number of phonemes or sounds in a word. Students manipulate the sounds by moving counters or tokens into each box as a spoken word is segmented into its individual sounds. Elkonin boxes can also be used to help students blend sounds together to form words.

This example works for SOL and SUN.

This example works for FROG and RANA.

The use of Elkonin Boxes is a fun and engaging way to build phonological awareness in English and Spanish. Teachers pronounce a word slowly, stretching it out by sounds. Students repeat and pronounce the word while moving a token into a box to represent the sound. This encourages students to listen for each individual sound in a word.

Let's take a look at what a cross-linguistic phonemic awareness lesson could look like in the classroom.

Key Terms

Phonological Awareness: The ability to recognize and manipulate sounds in a language.

Phonemic Awareness: A subcategory of phonological awareness that relates to identifying phonemes (the smallest units of sound) in a language.

Phonotactics: The permissible ways or patterns in which phonemes can or cannot be combined in a language.

In Action

Ms. Martínez, the Spanish-language teacher and Ms. Smith, the English Language Arts teacher, are coteaching in a dual-language Kindergarten program. They have already taught their students all the vowel sounds and most of the consonant sounds.

Both teachers engage students in various phonological-awareness activities such as rhyme recognition and chanting, as well as phonemic activities such as syllable counting, blending, and segmenting in each language during language arts time.

Their core language arts program in English and in Spanish includes sound-spelling cards and picture word cards that they use for instruction and display in their classroom.

Ms. Martínez and Ms. Smith teach cross-linguistic transfer of sounds using similar routines, rhymes, chants, and picture cards.

Spanish to English Lesson: Phonemic Awareness

Ms. Martínez will start by reviewing the target phoneme in Spanish and engaging students in word play and phonemic awareness activities. Then, using cognates, she will explicitly demonstrate that the sound **/n/** is the same in English and Spanish.

Paso 1: Repasar lo que ya sabemos y hemos aprendido en español		
Introducir la rima	Muestre la tarjeta ilustrada de nido. Diga con ritmo y prosodia: *Nido, nido* *No hagan ruido.*	
Reconocer y producir el sonido	Invite a los estudiantes a repetir con ritmo. *Escuchen este sonido: /n/.* *Díganlo conmigo: /n/.* *Díganlo solitos: /n/.* *Díganlo alto: /n/.* *Díganlo bajito: /n/.*	
Articulación del sonido	Motive a los estudiantes a observar detenidamente cómo se pronuncia el sonido /n/. *Cierren sus ojos.* *Pronuncien el sonido /n/.* *¿Dónde está su lengua?* *¿Están sus labios abiertos o cerrados?* *¿Sale aire de su boca?*	
Reconocimiento de palabras	*¿Qué palabras conocemos que comienzan con el sonido /n/?* *Escuchen estas palabas, repitan después de mi:* *naranja, nube, nopal, negro, niña.*	
Segmentar y contar sílabas	*Vamos a separar y contar las silabas de cada palabra.* *Escuchen esta palabra: naranja.* *Díganla conmigo: naranja.* *Separen las sílabas: na - ran - ja.* *Cuéntenlas conmigo: na - ran - ja.* *Tiene 3 sílabas.* Repita con las otras tarjetas ilustradas.	

Paso 2: Conectar y comparar con el inglés		
Establecer la relación de transferencia	*¿Creen que el sonido /n/ suena y se pronuncia igual en inglés que en español?* *Hoy vamos a aprender que el sonido /n/ suena igual y se pronuncia igual en español y en inglés.*	Español Inglés
Usar cognados para demostrar la relación positiva entre el sonido y letra en español y en inglés al inicio de cada palabra	Muestre cada una de las tarjetas ilustradas y diga la palabra en español enfatizando el sonido inicial /n/ mientras le pregunta a los estudiantes como se dice la palabra en inglés para conectar el sonido inicial /n/ en cada palabra. *Esta es una nota.* *¿Cómo se dice nota en inglés? (note)* *Este es el norte.* *¿Cómo se dice norte en inglés? (north)* *Estos son números.* *¿Cómo se dice números en inglés? (numbers)*	
Paso 3: Promover destrezas metalingüísticas al resumir lo aprendido		
Resumir lo aprendido	*¿Qué hemos aprendido hoy?* *Que el sonido /n/ suena y se pronuncia igual en español y en inglés.*	Español Inglés
Afirmar la lectoescritura bilingüe y las conexiones con el inglés	*Más tarde, la maestra Smith les va a enseñar más sobre el sonido /n/ en inglés. Pero ustedes le van a decir que ya saben que es igual en español y en inglés.*	

English to Spanish: Phonemic Awareness

Ms. Smith will continue the cross-linguistic transfer lesson in English and expand it by strategically pointing that not all words that start with the sound **/n/** are Spanish/English cognates.

Step 1: Review what we know and have learned in English		
Introduce the Rhyme	Playfully say this rhyme and have students repeat. *Nest, nest* *A great place to rest!*	
Recognize and Produce the Sound	*Listen to this sound: /n/.* *Say it with me: /n/.*	
Sound Articulation	Review and invite students to discern the articulation of the /n/ sound. *Pronounce the /n/ sound.* *Where is your tongue?* *Are your lips open or closed?* *Is air coming out of your mouth?* *Now what if you were to make the /n/ sound in Spanish?* *Would your tongue and lips be in the same place?* *Would air come out of your mouth?* *Let's try!* *Tell your partner what you think.*	
Word Recognition	Invite students to recall words that begin with the /n/ sound. *What words in English do we know that begin with the sound /n/?* *Listen to these words and repeat them after me: number, note, nine, nose, nut.*	9 1 2 3 4 5 6 7 8
Word Play: That's the One!	Play "That's the One! " by showing each picture card saying the name of the object, stressing the initial sound. Students identify the one that begins with the target sound /n/. Say: *I am going to say three words.* *Tell which one starts with the sound /n/.* *Dog, bed,* ***nine.*** *Red,* ***nut****, cat.* *Cow, box,* ***nest.***	9

Step 2: Connect and compare to Spanish		
Establish the Transfer Relationship and Extend Knowledge	*We know that the /n/ sound is pronounced the same way in Spanish. So do all words that start with the /n/ sound in English start with the /n/ sound in Spanish?*	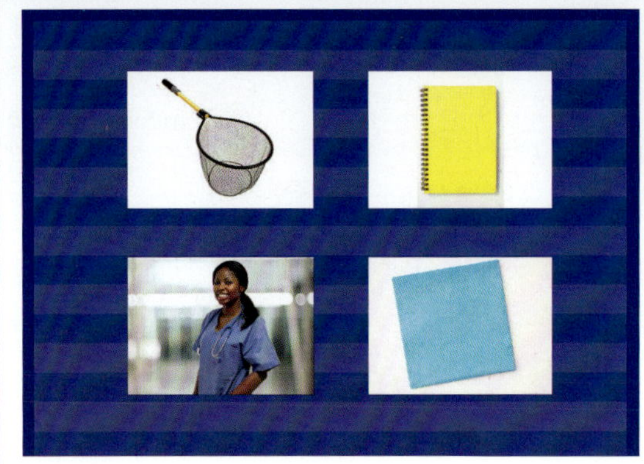
Demonstrate Noncognate Words with the Initial **/n/** Sound	*Now let's look at other words that start with the sound /n/ in English.* *This is a net.* *How do you say net in Spanish? (malla)* *This is a nurse.* *How do you say nurse in Spanish? (enfermera)* *This is a notebook.* *How do you say notebook in Spanish? (libreta)* *This is a napkin.* *How do you say napkin in Spanish? (servilleta)*	

Step 3: Promote metalinguistic skills by summarizing what has been learned		
Summarize the Learning Promote Metalinguistic Skills	*What did we learn today?* *We learned that the sound /n/ is pronounced the same in English and Spanish. Some words that start with the sound /n/ in English and Spanish mean the same thing.* *And we also learned that words with the same meaning can start with different sounds.*	 

Assessment Considerations

Phonological awareness assessments play a crucial role in early literacy development and can help educators tailor instruction to meet the specific needs of students. Assessing phonemic awareness in bilingual students requires careful consideration of their language development and proficiency in both languages.

There are important considerations when conducting phonological and phonemic awareness assessment with bilingual students:

1. Language proficiency and language dominance

Bilingual students may have different levels of proficiency in their native language and the partner language. Bilingual students may be more proficient in one language than the other, which can affect their phonemic awareness skills. Assess phonemic awareness in their dominant language first.

2. Phonological transfer

Be aware of the sound-transfer relationships between the partner languages. Encourage transfer of phonological features from one language to another. Teaching and assessing transferable sounds first will promote understanding and facilitate success.

3. Assessment tools

Use assessment tools that are appropriate for bilingual students. Ensure that the assessment materials include equitable tasks appropriate to the linguistic features of each language.

4. Age and developmental appropriateness

Consider the age and developmental stage of students. Phonemic awareness tasks should be age and developmentally appropriate in both languages.

5. Monitor progress over time in both languages

Progress and response to the various phonemic awareness tasks may differ in each language. Nontransferable sounds may be more difficult than transferable sounds. Administer the assessments separately, but view both languages as mutually reinforcing and analyze results side-by-side to document each student's biliteracy trajectory.

Pause and Reflect

What two strategies recommended in this chapter are you most excited to integrate into your instruction—and why?

Why is understanding syllabication a "fundamental skill" in both Spanish and English?

Conclusion

The musicality of a language is an essential aspect of communication and plays a role in conveying meaning, emotions, and emphasis, as well as making communication engaging. Phonology is an important part of the musicality of a language. As teachers of language learners, we teach the sounds of a language with joyous play while monitoring with understanding as students internalize, produce, and become familiar with the sound system of languages they make their own.

Cross-linguistic transfer of phonological and phonemic awareness is promoted through similarity of learning conditions such as routines, word play, rhymes, chants, Elkonin boxes, and phonemic awareness activities appropriate to the features of each language.

Teaching phonemic awareness for biliteracy also requires an understanding of the different phonotactics in each language, or the pattern of phoneme sequences such as syllabic structures, onset/rime, final consonants, and consonant clusters authentic to each language.

Monitoring and assessing phonological and phonemic awareness across languages entails an understanding of which sounds transfer and which do not. While each language is assessed separately, the results need to be analyzed together to discern the degree of cross-linguistic transfer occurring and the next instructional steps.

Key Takeaways

The prosody or musicality of a language plays a role in conveying meaning and in understanding the language and the culture of the people who speak it.

The syllable is the fundamental unit for understanding pronunciation, stress patterns, and word formation in Spanish. Phoneme identification and isolation is essential for English literacy. For all language learners, phonological awareness is an essential skill.

When the instructional methods and materials in one language context are similar to those in the other language context, the transfer of skills and knowledge from one language to the other is facilitated.

Language learners need to have a clear understanding of the meaning of the words they are segmenting or blending in both languages. The use of illustrations, manipulatives, and multisensory approaches is beneficial to internalizing the musicality of each language and supports comprehension.

Assessing phonological awareness in bilingual students requires a nuanced and individualized approach that considers their language proficiency, dominance, and developmental stage. It is essential to use appropriate assessment tools and to monitor progress in both languages to support students' literacy development effectively.

Chapter 6

Orthography

> "La ortografía es un reflejo de la evolución del idioma; al aprender sobre ella, aprendemos también algo de la historia y la lengua que hablamos y escribimos, con la que expresamos deseos, sentimientos, sueños, aspiraciones e ideas".
>
> *"Orthography is a reflection of the evolution of language; by learning about it, we also learn about its history and the language we speak and write, with which we express desires, feelings, dreams, aspirations, and ideas."*
>
> –Ada & Campoy, 2018

In the previous chapter, we took an in-depth look at phonology and its role in cross-linguistic instruction. Orthography and phonology are two different language subsystems, but they are closely interconnected because they both deal with language representation. Phonology explores the sound patterns of language, while orthography deals with the written representation of those sounds.

In this chapter, we look at orthography and instructional sequences for the cross-linguistic transfer connections that can be made between English and Spanish. A larger definition of orthography, one that goes beyond phonics instruction, is emphasized to show just how crucial this subsystem is for language learning, especially as it integrates with other subsystems to support writing. Direct and systematic instructional sequences for transferable and nontransferable sound-spelling relations will be explored.

In This Chapter

Orthography

Orthography comes from the Greek roots **ortho**, meaning "correct," and **graph**, meaning "writing," and it refers to the conventional spelling system of a language. It includes rules for spelling words, dividing words into syllables, and using punctuation marks. Orthography ensures consistency and standardization in written language, allowing people to communicate effectively and understand the intended meaning of words. Different languages have their own specific orthographic rules and conventions, and mastering these rules is essential for literacy and clear communication in written form.

Orthography can vary greatly across different languages and writing systems. For example, some languages, like Spanish and English, use a phonetic writing system where each symbol represents a specific sound. In this case, orthography is mapping sounds (phonemes) to print (graphemes or letters). Other languages, Mandarin Chinese for example, use a logographic or partial logographic writing system. In these cases, symbols represent entire words or morphemes.

The relationship between phonology and orthography can also vary significantly from one language to another. In languages with very regular or transparent orthographies, like Spanish, the relationship between phonemes (the individual sounds of the language) and graphemes (the written representation of sounds) is usually straightforward. Each sound is represented by a specific letter or combination of letters. However, in languages with more irregular or opaque orthographies, like English, the relationship between sounds and letters can be more complex. The same sound might be represented in different ways, or different sounds might be represented by the same letter or combination of letters.

Orthography Is Fundamental for Literacy

Orthography in all alphabetic languages plays a crucial role in literacy. It provides a standardized system of writing that represents spoken language and the symbolic representations of sounds (letters). This connection between sounds and symbols is fundamental for reading and writing.

This table shows some of the ways in which orthography is essential to literacy and language and how it connects to other language subsystems.

Language Subsystem	The Role of Orthography
Phonology	Orthography provides the visual representation of sounds. Understanding the relationship between letters and sounds (phonics) is essential for early literacy. Orthography helps in teaching this relationship systematically.
Morphology	Morphemes are the smallest unit of meaning in a word. The way words are spelled often reflects their morphological structure. Understanding how morphemes are spelled can provide insight into the meaning and usage of a word.
Semantics	Consistent orthography aids in quick word recognition, enhancing reading fluency. Knowing how words are spelled helps with recognizing words in various contexts and understanding their meanings, thus contributing to vocabulary building.
Grammar and Syntax	Orthography includes punctuation rules, which are essential for understanding the grammatical structure of sentences. Correct usage of punctuation marks is vital in written communication.
Pragmatics	Orthography plays a role in preserving languages by providing a written form, which is crucial for documenting cultural heritage. It is often tied to cultural and national identity, representing a community's unique linguistic characteristics.

Orthography serves as the foundation of literacy, enabling individuals to read, write, and communicate effectively. Furthermore, it provides consistent guidance for technological applications, such as text-to-speech and speech-to-text systems, in accurately converting written language into spoken words and thereby playing a pivotal role in education and society.

Orthography and Biliteracy

Orthography plays a significant role in biliteracy. Proficiency in the orthography of one language can facilitate the learning of a second language. Similarities in alphabets or writing systems such as in Spanish and English can lead to positive transfer, where knowledge of the sound-spelling relationships in one language helps in learning another.

Proficiency in both languages' orthographies supports academic success, allowing students to excel in reading, writing, and overall language-related tasks in different educational contexts. In addition, it can lead to enhanced cognitive flexibility, allowing individuals to switch between different sound-spelling systems, recognize diverse patterns, and understand varying language structures.

Competence in the orthography of two languages also supports effective communication within diverse social and cultural settings, fostering understanding and collaboration. It is through orthography, or the way a word is written, that we know where it comes from, how it was first used, and how it may be currently used in various contexts. Orthography helps in preserving the written forms of languages, allowing communities to maintain their linguistic heritage and cultural identity.

In other words, orthography serves as the foundation for biliteracy by providing the necessary tools and skills to read and write proficiently in two languages. It enhances cognitive abilities, educational achievements, and social interactions, enabling individuals to navigate various linguistic and cultural contexts with confidence and competence.

Cross-Linguistic Connections

In English and Spanish, letter-sound correspondences are taught in an explicit systematic instructional sequence using manipulatives and high levels of student engagement and interaction. Segmenting and blending are explicitly practiced each day with meaningful practice and spiral review.

To support students who are acquiring new sounds and letters in a new language, it is important to map out which sounds and letters are familiar to students, the extent to which the sounds and letters are familiar, and which sounds and letters are new and unfamiliar (Cejas et al., 2018).

While understanding the close relationship between phonological awareness, phonics, and word recognition, instruction for biliteracy considers the transferability of sound-spelling correspondences across languages. These relationships in English and Spanish can be fully transferable, partially transferable, or nontransferable.

Orthography is foundational for biliteracy.

Caveat

The relationship between orthography and meaning is multifaceted. Spelling conventions can provide phonetic, morphological, historical, and even visual information that contributes to the overall meaning of words.

In a dual-language or bilingual instructional context, meaning is emphasized because meaning and cognitive associations help us internalize and learn language. The relationship between codifying, decoding, and encoding is always meaning-based.

Codifying

the process of negotiating, applying, and understanding the meaning of a word

Decoding

the process of blending and segmenting sounds in words to ascertain meaning

Encoding

the process of turning thoughts or the spoken word into writing for meaningful communication

Learn More

Lado, R. (1957). A comparison of the sound systems of English and Spanish. *Acta Lingüística, 11*(1), 23–29.

Urow, C., & Beeman, K. (2014). *El dictado*. Center for Teaching for Biliteracy. Adapted from the work of Kathy Escamilla and Literacy Squared. Retrieved from www.teachingforbiliteracy.com/wp-content/uploads/2014/09/The-Dictado.pdf

Martínez, R. B., & Fillmore, L. W. (2023). On curriculum and pedagogy in dual language bilingual education. In J. A. Freire, C. Alfaro, & E. de Jong, (Eds.), *The handbook of bilingual education*. Routledge.

- **Fully transferable:** sound-spellings are equivalent in Spanish and English, such as the **/m/** spelled **m**.
- **Partially transferable:** sound-spellings may represent the same sound in English and Spanish; however, the spelling may differ, for example **/k/** spelled **que** and **qui** in Spanish.
- **Nontransferable:** sound-spellings have the same spelling but not the same sound; for example, the letter **h** is silent in Spanish, but in English the letter **h** is pronounced **/h/**.

Note that the pronunciation of some letters in English and in Spanish can vary based on regional accents and sociocultural influences. The generalizations and rationales presented in the related charts on the pages that follow may not apply to every dialect or regional environment.

Fully Transferable Sound-Spelling Relations

There are many sound-spelling correspondences in Spanish that are directly transferable to English. This means that students who can recognize these sound-spellings in Spanish have a strong foundation for learning English phonics. As teachers introduce Spanish readers to English phonics, they can draw on many phonics elements that are common to both languages.

Fully Transferable Sound-Spelling Correspondences			
/b/ spelled b	/n/ spelled n	/g/ spelled g in ga, go, gu	l-blends (bl, cl, fl, gl, pl)
/d/ spelled d	/p/ spelled p	/g/ spelled gu in gue, gui	r-blends (br, cr, dr, fr, gr, pr, tr)
/f/ spelled f	/t/ spelled t	/k/ spelled c in ca, co, cu	diphthong /oi/ spelled oi, oy
/l/ spelled l	/y/ spelled y	/s/ spelled s and c in ce, ci	dipthong /ch/ spelled ch
/m/ spelled m	/ch/ spelled ch		

Key Terms

Phonetic Writing System: An orthographic system in which each symbol represents a specific sound.

Logographic or Partial Logographic Writing System: An orthographic system in which symbols may represent entire words or morphemes.

Nontransferable Sound-Spelling Relations

Some sound-spelling correspondences between Spanish and English are nontransferable. This means that students will need explicit instruction that identifies these differences across languages. The chart in these pages outlines some of these nontransferable relations.

Spanish		Letter	English	
Sound	**Details**	**Spelling**	**Sound**	**Details**
/a/ /e/ /i/ /o/ /u/	Five main vowel sounds map into five corresponding graphemes (letters) consistently. Vowels pair to form diphthongs or hiatus (hiatos) without changing their individual sounds. An orthographic accentuation mark is applied only to vowels and to signal a stressed pronunciation. The letter Yy sounding /i/ is sometimes considered a vowel.	Aa Ee Ii Oo Uu Yy	/ă/ /ā/ /ĕ/ /ē/ /ĭ/ /ī/ /ŏ/ /ō/ /ŭ/ /ū/	These five vowels are produced and represented by a combination of single vowels with short and long sounds. Vowel pairs in English may form digraphs—two vowels together that form one sound. There is no orthographic accentuation mark to signal stressed pronunciation. Yy is a consonant letter if at the beginning of a word or syllable. In any other placement it is a vowel.
/g/ /j/	G makes the /g/ sound for: syllables ga, go, gu and for gue, gui as in gato and guiso. When G is followed by letter u, the u sound is silent. G makes the /j/ sound for: syllables ge and gi, as in gema and girasol.	Gg	/j/	G makes the /j/ sound when: followed by an e at the beginning or end of a word: gem, page followed by an i: ginger, giraffe used as dg spelling at the end of a syllable when following a short vowel sound: bridge, edge
N/A	H is silent in Spanish.	Hh	/h/	The /h/ sound in English occurs only at the beginning of a syllable and never as the final sound in a word. When not in the first syllable, it is paired with a consonant ch, gh, rh, ph, sh, th, or wh.
/j/	The sound /j/ is spelled with a j: jugo, jungla, jazmín. The sound /j/ is spelled with a g when followed by e or i, as in gema and girasol.	Jj	/dʒ/	In English, j represents the English sound /dʒ/: juice, jungle, jazmín

Spanish		Letter	English	
Sound	**Details**	**Spelling**	**Sound**	**Details**
/k/	The q is always followed by the silent u to form syllables que and qui.	Qq	/kw/	This is always spelled qu in English: queen, liquid.
/rr/ /r/	The Rr is forcibly doubled at the beginning of words and when doubled in the middle of words as in digraph rr. /r/ has a softer pronunciation in the middle of words.	Rr	/rw/ /r/	/rw/ as in rabbit and right is not pronounced in Spanish. Medial consonant doubling maintains a soft /r/ sound: arrow.
/b/	The Vv is pronounced /b/ in Spanish: volcán, vapor, violín.	Vv	/v/	The letter v is always followed by a vowel: vet, vapor, vision.
/s/ /ks/ /j/	The letter Xx represents three sounds in Spanish: /s/ when x is at the beginning of a word: xilófono /ks/ at the end of a word—Félix, clímax—or between vowels éxito /j/ in words like México, and Ximena	Xx	/ks/ /z/ /g/	The letter x represents three sounds in English: /ks/ when preceded by a vowel /z/ as in xylophone /g/ as in exhibit
/y/	The "double l" is a a consonant digraph pronounced /y/: llamo, llave lluvia, llora.	Ll	/l/	This is more frequently used as a double ll at the end of a syllable, as in yellow, and after a short vowel, as in bell.
/s/ /z/	The z is often pronounced /s/. The "seseo" is when ci plus ce or s are pronounced /z/.	Zz	/z/	This is the initial sound in zoo, zero, zoom. This is subject to medial consonant doubling, as in puzzle, dizzy, fuzzy. This is often found at the end of a word or syllable: ooze, haze.

Zero-Transfer Sound-Spelling Relations

Some sound-spelling correspondences between Spanish and English have zero transfer. Like nontransferable relations, students will need explicit instruction that identifies these differences across languages. The chart below outlines some of these zero relations.

Spanish Sound-Spellings That Do Not Apply to English
ñ
ü diéresis
á é í ó ú accents
English Sound-Spellings That Do Not Apply to Spanish
All short vowels and the schwa
Long vowels with silent e
Long-vowel digraphs
Double vowel diphthongs except oy and oi
Digraphs sh, th, wh, ph, gh, ng
s-blends
Final consonant blends
Three-letter consonant blends

Syllabic Pattern Comparisons

In both Spanish and English, syllables are a units of sound that form the basic building blocks of a word. Each syllable in a word must contain a vowel or vowel combination.

In spoken language, syllables are produced through the modulation of pitch, loudness, and duration of sounds. Listeners perceive the rhythm and flow of speech based on the arrangement of these syllables.

In written language, syllables are represented graphically on the page. The number of letters or characters in a word may not always correspond directly to the number of syllables, as some letters may represent multiple sounds, some may be silent, or some sounds may be represented by combinations of letters.

While both spoken and written syllables in Spanish and English involve the concept of breaking down words into smaller units, the way they are perceived and represented differs due to the distinct nature of oral and written communication. Additionally, the relationship between spoken and written syllables can vary based on the language and writing system.

Syllabic patterns in Spanish and English exhibit some differences due to variations in their phonological structures. Spanish is a multisyllabic language, where most words have three or more syllables. English is mostly a monosyllabic language where most words have one syllable. Multisyllabic words in English usually derive from Latin, Greek, or French languages.

Here are some general syllabic pattern comparisons.

Feature	Spanish	English
Regularity	There is a regular and consistent syllabic pattern.	This may vary significantly based on factors such as word origin, surrounding sounds, and stress patterns.
Vowel Pronunciation	Vowels are pronounced consistently.	There is variability in pronunciation due to factors like vowel reduction and the influence of surrounding consonants. There is a prevalence of diphthongs where vowels combine to form a single sound.
Consonant Pronunciation	Consonants are pronounced consistently.	The same combination of consonants can be pronounced differently in various words and contexts. Pronunciation is influenced by the position of a consonant(s) in a word or the proximity to other sounds.
Syllable Stress	Spanish is a syllable-timed language. Syllables are pronounced at an even pace. In about 77 percent of words, stress is placed in the penultimate (second to last) syllable. Accentuation marks indicate syllabic stress.	English is a stress-timed language. Stressed syllables are pronounced at a more regular pace; an unstressed syllable may be shortened.

As the table suggests, Spanish tends to have a more regular and consistent syllabic pattern, while English exhibits greater variability due to its stress-timed nature and the influence of factors like vowel reduction and consonant clusters.

In both Spanish and English, syllables play a crucial role in literacy. Syllables establish the phonetic and orthographic structure of words. Understanding syllables helps learners identify the stressed syllable, which is important for proper pronunciation and word stress. Knowing how to break down words into syllables is essential for reading and writing.

Additionally, in Spanish, this knowledge helps readers to decode and pronounce words accurately. Understanding syllables helps Spanish learners identify the stressed syllable, which is important for proper pronunciation and word stress. This is crucial for applying accent rules correctly. Furthermore, knowing how to break words into syllables enhances reading fluency. It enables emergent Spanish readers to process multisyllabic words (*pelota, zapato, mariposa*) in smaller, manageable chunks, making them easier to recognize and understand their meaning.

This comparison suggests the most common syllabic patterns organized from most to least frequent.

Spanish	
V	a, o, a-mo, u-na
CV	mi, la, ca-sa, me-sa, to-ma-te
CVC	sol, mar, can-ta, mi-rar
VC	el, un, ar-co, is-la
CCV	glo-bo, cla-ro, i-glú
CCVC	flor, tren, a-trac-ti-vo
CVCC	cons-tan-te
CCVCC	trans-por-te

English	
CVC	mat, pet, dig
VC	at, in, up
CV	go, no, be
CVCe	make, time, mule
CVVC	mail, seat, book
r controlled	mart, chart
consonant+le	ta-ble, un-cle
CCCVC	string, split, strap

Punctuation Marks

Spanish and English punctuation marks share many similarities, but there are some differences in their usage and appearance. Here's a brief comparison of the most common punctuation marks in both languages.

Spanish	English
Punto (.) Used to end sentences	**Period (.)** Used to end sentences
Puntos suspensivos (...) Used to express suspense, doubt, or continuation; used to indicates that words have been excluded	**Ellipses (...)** Used to express suspense, doubt, or continuation; used to indicate that words have been excluded
Coma (,) Used to separate items in a list, clauses in a sentence, or phrases	**Comma (,)** Used to separate items in a list, clauses in a sentence, or phrases; used after the greeting in friendly letters
Signos de interrogación (¿?) Used at the beginning and end of a question	**Question mark (?)** Used at the end of a question
Signos de exclamación (¡!) Used at the beginning and the end of an exclamatory statement	**Exclamation mark (!)** Used at the end an exclamatory statement
Comillas (" ") or (« ») Used for quotes, titles or direct thoughts in literary works	**Quotation marks (" ")** Used to indicate direct speech, quotes, or titles
Dos puntos (:) Used to introduce a list or an explanation; used after the greeting in a letter	**Colon (:)** Used to introduce a list or an explanation
Punto y coma (;) Used to separate independent clauses or items in a list where commas have already been used	**Semicolon (;)** Used to separate independent clauses or items in a list where commas have already been used
Guion Corto o Rayita (-) Used to separate words, to indicate prefixes, suffixes, and syllables; used to mark dates	**Hyphen (-)** Used to separate words; used to indicate prefixes, suffixes, and syllables; used to mark dates
Guion Largo o Raya (–) Used to the open and close a dialogue; used to enclose clarifications or incises	**Dash (–)** Used to indicate a pause, set off information within a sentence, or to indicate a range of numbers
Apóstrofo Used to join two words to indicate the elision of sounds, usually a vowel	**Apostrophe** Used to show a missing letter or contraction; used to indicate possession in English only
Paréntesis ( ) corchetes [ ] llaves { } Used in pairs to separate or intersperse one text within another or to make a clarification	**Parentheses ( ) Brackets [ ] braces { }** Used in pairs to separate or intersperse one text within another or to make a clarification

When teachers understand the similarities and differences between the two languages, they are able to plan and deliver instruction that facilitates and supports cross-linguistic transfer. Some students may recognize similarities and differences between languages on their own, making an intuitive leap by applying what they know about their known language to the new language. However, rather than leaving this linguistic transfer up to chance, or leaving room for potential approximations to be made, cross-linguistic transfer must be intentionally and strategically taught. Explicit teaching for linguistic transfer builds a deeper knowledge about the shared elements as well as the unique features of each language and how each language works.

By intentionally providing a comprehensible connection between languages, teachers guide students to become more strategic thinkers. As students think about the languages they are using and learning, they develop the metacognitive skills and metalinguistic knowledge needed for proficient biliteracy.

“Rather than leaving this linguistic transfer up to chance, or leaving room for potential approximations to be made, cross-linguistic transfer must be intentionally and strategically taught.”

 |

In Action

A key goal of these cross-linguistic lessons is for students to establish sound-to-print correlations at the letter level, but to also be able to internalize a bank of words they can associate with the sound-spelling relationships in each language.

Spanish to English Lesson: Sound-Spelling Connections Dd

Ms. Martínez has already introduced the sound **/d/**, represented by letter **Dd** to her dual-language Kindergarten students. During the bridging lesson, Ms. Martínez used picture cards to review images of objects that start with the sound **/d/** in Spanish. These images help students name each object and recognize the meaning. Mrs. Martínez also showed cognate picture cards to establish the Spanish-English transferable sound-spelling relation of **/d/** across languages.

Next, Ms. Martínez shows the spelling of each word that correlates to each image, to affirm word meaning and support sound-to-print recognition. Students will engage in speaking and hands-on activities where they practice and demonstrate word-to-image as well as sound-to-letter recognition. Students will also have an opportunity to negotiate meaning and discern words that begin with the target sound in Spanish but do not begin with the target sound in English. Ample opportunity for oracy and negotiation of meaning is provided to promote prior knowledge and language internalization.

Remember that this is not a phonics lesson. It is a cross-linguistic transfer lesson, where students connect, compare, and contrast the sound-spelling relationships in words across languages. Comprehensive phonics instruction has already taken place in each of the Spanish Language Arts and English Language Arts classrooms.

Paso 1: Usar lo que ya sabemos y hemos aprendido en español		
Repasar la correlación de sonido y letra Establecer la relación de transferencia	Muestre la tarjeta de sonido-letra de la Dd en español. Invite a los estudiantes a responder a coro. *¿Qué sonido hace esta letra?* *¿Cómo se llama esta letra?* Muestre la tarjeta de sonido-letra de la Dd en inglés. *¿Qué sonido hace esta letra en inglés?* *¿Cómo se llama esta letra en inglés?* Señale el borde verde en ambas tarjetas. *¿Tiene un borde verde?* *¿Qué quiere decir esto?* *Sí, el borde verde quiere decir que la letra Dd representa el sonido /d/ tanto en español como en inglés.* *Miren las letras _ed en la tarjeta de inglés. Las letras _ed se pronuncian /d/ al final de algunas palabras en inglés como played, learned, cleaned.*	
Reconocer y nombrar palabras usando imágenes Promueva conocimientos previos y asociaciones Invite a los estudiantes a conversar con un compañero	Muestre tarjetas de imágenes. (dado, dedo, dibujo, doce, durazno) Invite a los estudiantes a dividir las palabras por sus sílabas. Por ejemplo señale la tarjeta y pregunte: *¿Qué es esto?* un dado *Separen por sílabas:* da-do *¿Qué palabra?* dado Promueva el diálogo entre pares de estudiantes. *¿Qué es un ___?* *¿Para qué sirve?* *¿Quién usa un/una___?* *¿Dónde has visto un/una__?*	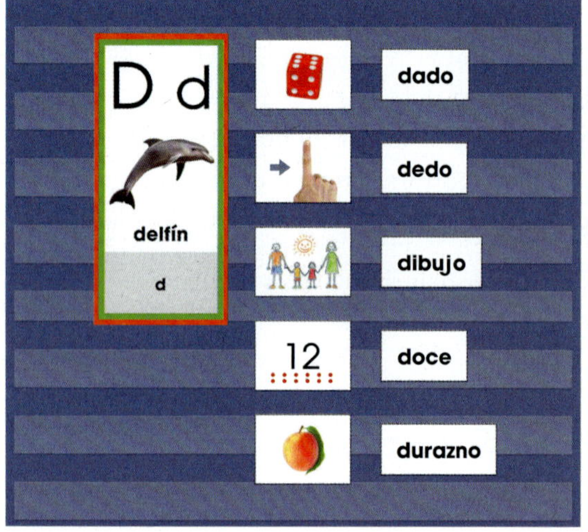

Señalar y comparar cognados y la correlación del fonema inicial en español y en inglés	Muestre la tarjeta de sonido y letra en inglés. *¿Qué sonido representa esta letra?* *¿Como se llama esta letra en inglés?* Muestre imágenes de palabras que comienzan con Dd en ambos idiomas. Luego invite a los estudiantes a nombrar cada palabra en español y en inglés. *Esta palabra en español es: _____* *¿Cómo se dice en inglés?: _____* Señale y compare la correlación de sonido y letra al inicio de cada palabra en español y en inglés. *Todas estas palabras comienzan con el sonido /d/ y la letra Dd en español y en inglés.*	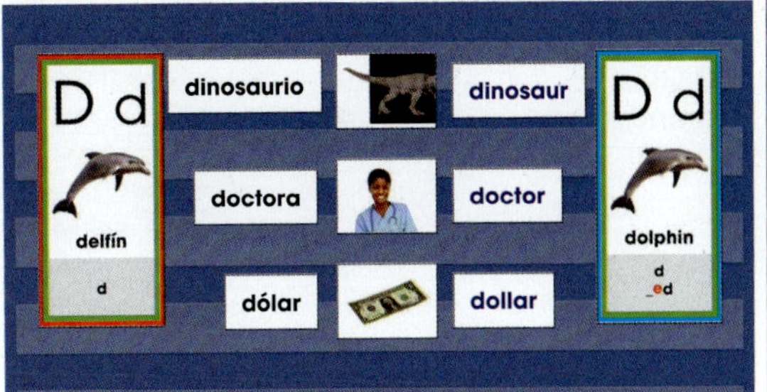

Paso 2: Conectar, comparar y contrastar con el inglés

Practicar oralidad y demostrar reconocimiento de sonido, letra y palabra tanto en español como en inglés	Reparta las tarjetas de imágenes y las tarjetas de palabras. Entre compañeros los estudiantes podrán: • emparejar cada imagen con las palabras correspondientes • preguntarle a un compañero: *¿Cómo se dice ___ en inglés?*	

Paso 3: Promover destrezas metalingüísticas al resumir lo aprendido		
Resumir lo aprendido	Promueva destrezas metalingüísticas al preguntar: *¿Qué hemos aprendido hoy?* *Hemos aprendido que el sonido /d/ y la letra Dd se pronuncia igual en español y en inglés.* *Que algunas palabras que comienzan con /d/ en español también comienzan con /d/ en inglés.* *Las palabras que significan lo mismo y se escriben casi igual en inglés y en español se llaman cognados.* *Que no todas las palabras que comienzan con /d/ en español comienzan con /d/ en inglés.*	
Afirmar la lectoescritura bilingüe y las conexiones con el inglés	*Más tarde, la maestra de inglés (Ms. Smith) les va a enseñar más palabras en inglés que comienzan con el sonido y la letra Dd. ¡Ustedes son bilingües y están aprendiendo el sonido de las letras en español y en inglés!*	

English to Spanish Lesson: Sound-Spelling Connections Dd

During the English bridging time, Ms. Smith reminds students that they have already studied the sound and the letter **Dd** in Spanish and have already established the positive transfer relationship with a quick review. She will then expand the lesson beyond the cognate picture cards to include the picture cards of images and words that begin with **Dd** in English.

The lesson from English to Spanish follows the same steps. This will assure the similarity of routines and learning conditions that promote cross-linguistic transfer. However, the image and word examples to represent the sound-spelling relationship in English and the engagement activities will differ.

Remember that cross-linguistic transfer is bidirectional. This means that it does not matter if a concept is first introduced in English or Spanish. The key feature of the cross-linguistic transfer lesson is to bridge or connect the concepts from one language to another and to affirm what was learned about each language as students engage in comparing and contrasting at the sound, letter, and word levels.

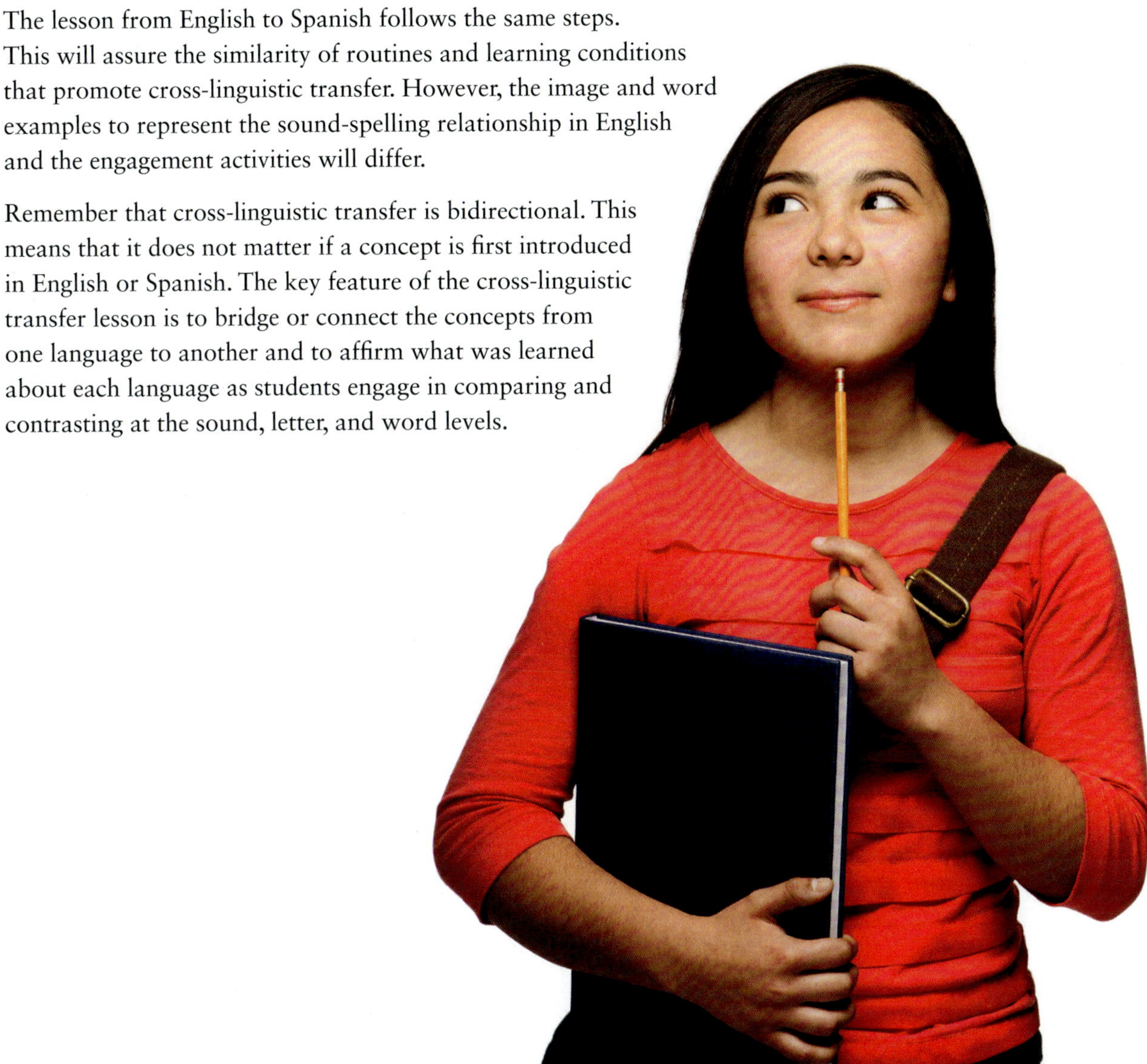

Step 1: Review what we know and have learned in English		
Review Sound-Letter Correlation Establish Transfer Relationship	Display a Dd sound-letter card in English. Invite students to respond in chorus. *What sound does this letter make?* *What is this letter called?* *What does this mean?* Next, display a Spanish Dd sound letter card. *What do you already know about the sound /d/ and the letter Dd in English and Spanish?* *Yes, the letter Dd represents the /d/ sound, and it is pronounced the same in both Spanish and English. Notice the letters -ed on the card. This means that in English the letters -ed at the end of some words are pronounced /d/ as in played, learned, and cleaned.*	D d dolphin d _ed
Recognize and Name Words Using Pictures Promote Prior Knowledge and Associations Invite Students to Converse with a Partner	Show images of words that start with the sound /d/. Promote dialogue between pairs of students. *What is a _____?* *What is it for?* *Who uses a _____?* *Where have you seen a _____?*	D d dolphin d _ed deer dog duck doctor dollar dinosaur

Point out the Correlation of Sound and Letter at the Beginning of Each Word	Point out the sound-letter correlation at the beginning of each word. Invite students to repeat the /d/ sound and name each word. *All these words begin with initial /d/ sound in English.* Point to each picture, and then point to the word. Pronounce the /d/ sound several times, then say the whole word. */d/ /d/ /d/ /d/ deer*	

Step 2: Connect, compare and contrast to Spanish		
Practice Oracy to Demonstrate Recognition of Sound, Letter, and Word Recognition in Both Spanish and English	Hand out picture cards and word cards in English and Spanish. In pairs student can: Create pictorial dictionaries in English and Spanish. Use word cards in a sentence using prompt frames: *A _____ is _____.* *A _____ has _____.* *A _____ can _____.* *Un _____ tiene _____.* *Un _____ puede _____.*	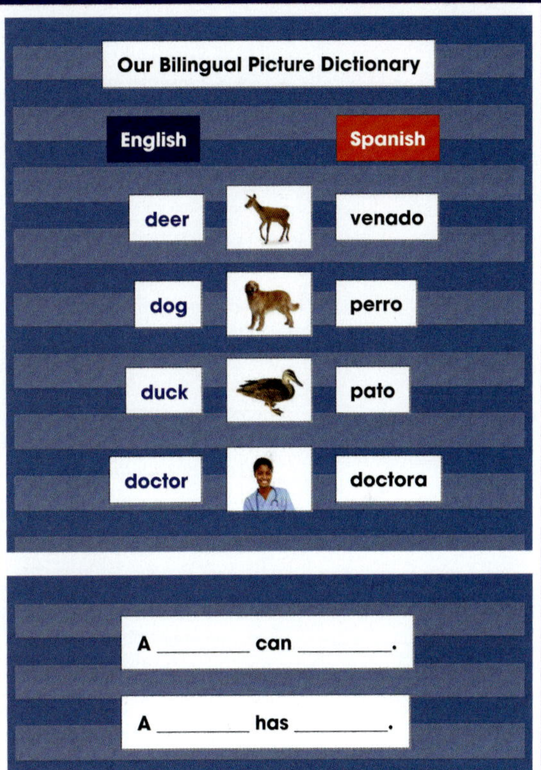

Step 3: Promote metalinguistic skills by summarizing what was learned		
Summarize What Was Learned	Promote metalinguistic skills by asking questions: *What have we learned today?* *We have learned that the /d/ sound and the letter Dd are pronounced the same in English and Spanish.* *Some words that begin with Dd in English also begin with Dd in Spanish. Words that mean the same and are spelled the same in English and Spanish are cognates.* *We also learned that some words that begin with the /d/ sound and the letter Dd in English do not begin with a Dd in Spanish.*	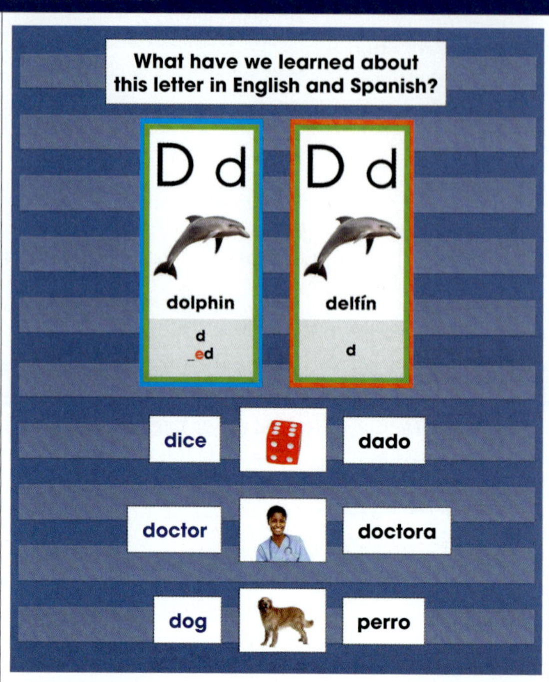
Affirm Biliteracy and Connections to Spanish	*Now you know and can use words that start with the sound /d/ and letter Dd in English as well as in Spanish.* *Turn to your partner and say three words you know that begin with Dd in English and Spanish.*	

Assessment Considerations

Whether implementing a sequential or a simultaneous approach to biliteracy, the order and organization of learning objectives and activities affects the way the information is processed and retained. Assessment of cross-linguistic sound-spelling relationships is sequential, systematic, bidirectional, and organized using a simple to complex sequence. It can be easily correlated to the scope and sequence of most comprehensive core language arts programs. The key to assessment for cross-linguistic transfer is to begin assessment with the transferable sound-spellings before the nontransferable sound-spellings.

Transferable Sound-Spellings	Nontransferable Sound-Spellings	English-Specific Sound-Spellings
Transferable consonants	Vowels	Vowel digraphs (long vowels, English)
Consonant digraphs	Diphthongs (Spanish)	Consonant digraphs
Consonant blends	Nontransferable consonants	Consonant clusters
		r-controlled
		Silent letters

Cross-Linguistic Sound-Spelling Inventory

Teachers can monitor students' biliteracy development by evaluating sound-spelling recognition in both English and Spanish using a Cross-Linguistic Sound-Spelling Inventory Record. A well-planned Cross-Linguistic Sound-Spelling Inventory includes letter names, sound recognition, and sample word identification. This inventory correlates to a scope and sequence continuum for transfer and enables monitoring and recording each student's progress toward biliteracy.

Sequential and Simultaneous Biliteracy

A sequential approach to biliteracy involves learning to read and write in one language before acquiring literacy skills in a second language. Dual-language 90/10 programs implement a sequential approach to biliteracy instruction.

A simultaneous approach to biliteracy involves learning to read and write in both languages at the same time. Dual-language 50/50 programs utilize a simultaneous approach to biliteracy instruction.

This inventory is given on an individual basis. Each language is assessed at a separate time. Students are assessed on sound-spellings that have already been taught for transfer, in addition to the letter name and sound, and they are asked to say a word that begins with the sound. Here are some sample cross-linguistic transfer inventories from Benchmark Education's *Sound-Spelling Transfer Kit*.

Cross-Linguistic Sound-Spelling Inventory Record

Level A: Transferable Sound-Spellings

Student Name:______________________ Grade: ______ Teacher: ______________________

Spanish				
Transferable Sound-Spelling Recognition				
Date	**Consonants and Vowels**	**Letter Name**	**Letter Sound**	**Word Example**
	Bb			
	Cc /k/			
	Cc /s/			
	Dd			
	Ff			
	Gg (ga, go, gu)			
	Kk			
	Ll			
	Mm			
	Nn			
	Pp			
	Ss			
	Tt			
	Ww			
	Yy			
	diphthong /oi/			
	digraph ch			
	l-blends			
	r-blends			

English				
Transferable Sound-Spelling Recognition				
Date	**Consonants and Vowels**	**Letter Name**	**Letter Sound**	**Word Example**
	Bb			
	Cc /k/			
	Cc /s/			
	Dd			
	Ff			
	Gg (hard)			
	Kk			
	Ll			
	Mm			
	Nn			
	Pp			
	Ss			
	Tt			
	Ww			
	Yy			
	diphthong /oi/			
	digraph ch			
	l-blends			
	r-blends			

Notes:

© Benchmark Education Company, LLC　　English-Spanish Sound-Spelling Transfer　1

Transferable sound-spellings

Cross-Linguistic Sound-Spelling Inventory Record

Level B: Non-Transferable Sound-Spellings

Student Name:______________________ Grade: ______ Teacher: ______________________

Spanish				
Non-Transferable Sound-Spelling Recognition				
Date	**Consonants and Vowels**	**Letter Name**	**Letter Sound**	**Word Example**
	Aa			
	Ee			
	Ii			
	Oo			
	Uu			
	Gg			
	Hh			
	Jj			
	Qq			
	Rr			
	Xx			
	Zz			
	Ñn			
	ll			
	rr			

Date	**Spanish Diphthongs**		**Sound**	**Word Example**
	ai	ay		
	au			
	ei	ey		
	eu			
	ia			
	ie			
	io			
	iu			
	ua			
	ue			
	ui	uy		
	uo			
	güe	güi		

English				
Non-Transferable Sound-Spelling Recognition				
Date	**Consonants and Vowels**	**Letter Name**	**Letter Sound**	**Word Example**
	Short a			
	Short e			
	Short i			
	Short o			
	Short u			
	Gg (soft)			
	Hh			
	Jj			
	Qq			
	Rr			
	Xx			
	Zz			

Notes:

2　English-Spanish Sound-Spelling Transfer　　© Benchmark Education Company, LLC

Nontransferable sound-spellings

Using the Results

Once a set of letters has been assessed in one language, the same letters are assessed in the other language. By taking the inventory in both languages and noting them in the same record, teachers will be able to monitor students' trajectories and reinforce instruction as needed in each language. They will have evidence for what a student already knows in each language and will be able to correlate the student's knowledge in one language to the other. The correlated records will affirm the student's cross-linguistic knowledge and reveal gaps that can be addressed.

Dictado

Dictado is an integrated approach to spelling (spelling, punctuation, syntax and grammar) used predominantly in Spanish literacy instruction (Escamilla et al., 2014). Instead of spelling one word at a time in Kindergarten and Grade 1, the dictado involves the dictation of a whole sentence. At the upper primary grades, dictado uses connected text. Words in the dictado sentence include high-frequency words and words containing the specific phonetical element that has been explicitly studied. All words come from the texts studied during the week. Teachers may choose from both options: the dictado or the single-word spelling approach associated with English spelling.

Dictation in a cross-linguistic lesson context is more like a shared learning activity than a test. Its purpose is to affirm the relationship between sounds, letters, word meaning, and word order. Dictation helps students become independent writers and teaches them to self-correct as they apply their metalinguistic knowledge across languages.

Mora and Dorta-Duque de Reyes (in press) examined cross-linguistic spelling approximations and identified categories that are very useful in evaluating students' generalizations across languages as they apply their emerging knowledge of sound-spelling relationships in each language. The errors or approximations represent students' efforts as they draw upon what they know to transcribe phonemes to the target language.

Category	Spanish Approximation to English		English Approximation to Spanish	
L1 Spelling Applied to L2	meik cald	for *make* for *called*	teene hugando	for *tiene* for *jugando*
Absent Phonemes	cach initing	for *catch* for *anything*	stand patendo	for *están* for *pateando*
Phoneme Collapse	ting finich	for *thing* for *finished*	plieyra escula	for *playera* for *escuela*
Unfamiliar Spelling Patterns	dos lern	for *does* for *learn*	parcke wevo	for *parque* for *huevo*
Word Boundaries	aplejus haftogo	for *apple juice* for *have to go*	earala sistan	for *ir a la* for *si están*
L1 Substitutions	la house the mesa	for *the house* for *the table*	pants de my mom's	for *pantalones* for *de mi mamá*

Cross-Linguistic Approximation Categories and Examples (Mora, 2001; Mora, 2016; Mora & Dorta-Duque de Reyes, in press).

Cross-Linguistic Approximation Categories and Examples

Teachers in a biliteracy classroom or teachers working in a dual collaboration can use the cross-linguistic spelling approximation categories to analyze students' metalinguistic understanding and progress toward decoding and encoding in two languages.

Class results can be tallied to discern high-percentage errors to reteach during whole-class sessions. Individual student dictation samples can be annotated using the cross-linguistic spelling approximations and collected periodically to show evidence of growth over time.

Cross-Linguistic Spelling Approximation Inventory Individual Record

Student Name:______________________________Grade: ______ Teacher: ____________________

Date:	Categories	Date:
Spanish to English		**English to Spanish**
	L1 Spelling Applied to L2	
	Absent Phonemes	
	Phoneme Collapse	
	Unfamiliar Spelling Patterns	
	Word Boundaries	
	L1 Substitutions	

Pause and Reflect

What are three to five key considerations when planning cross-linguistic instruction that builds students' orthography skills?

How might you use a Cross-Linguistic Sound-Spelling Inventory to monitor student progress and inform instruction?

Conclusion

Orthography is the standardized system of writing in alphabetic languages. It serves as a fundamental pillar of literacy, bridging the gap between spoken language and written representation. The relationship between phonology and orthography varies across languages, with regular orthographies like Spanish offering straightforward sound-symbol correspondence, while irregular ones like English present complex patterns.

Proficiency in a language's orthography not only aids in mastering that language, but also facilitates the learning of a second language, particularly when similarities exist between writing systems as they do in Spanish and English. This proficiency enhances academic success and cognitive flexibility, enabling individuals to navigate diverse sound-spelling systems and understand complex language structures.

The interplay between orthography and meaning is intricate, as spelling conventions contribute phonetic, morphological, historical, and visual cues to word meanings. In bilingual contexts, emphasis on meaning and cognitive associations fosters effective language internalization. Cross-linguistic transfer instruction that leads to understanding of linguistic similarities and differences between the sound-spelling systems of two different languages is essential for the development of proficient biliteracy. Moreover, by establishing comprehensible connections between languages, teachers empower students to develop metacognitive skills and metalinguistic knowledge essential for skilled bilingualism.

Assessment in cross-linguistic instruction follows a systematic approach, focusing on transferable sound-spellings to nontransferable ones. A well-designed Cross-Linguistic Sound-Spelling Inventory, encompassing letter recognition, sound identification, and word comprehension, enables monitoring and recording of students' progress toward biliteracy.

In essence, the deliberate integration of orthographic knowledge, meaningful associations, and strategic instruction equips students with the tools needed to excel in both languages—and fosters a generation of proficient and confident bilingual learners.

Key Takeaways

Regular or transparent orthographies like that of Spanish offer a straightforward sound-symbol correspondence, while irregular or opaque ones like English present complex sound-symbol patterns.

Proficiency in one language's orthography can facilitate proficiency in a partner language, fostering academic success and cognitive flexibility.

Spelling conventions contribute phonetic, morphological, historical, and visual cues to word meanings.

In bilingual contexts, emphasis on meaning and cognitive associations fosters effective language internalization.

Assessment of orthography follows a systematic approach, focusing on transferable sound-spellings to nontransferable ones.

elephant
photosynthesis
ten
eleven
11
12
13
fourteen
14
fifteen
15
sixteen
16
seventeen
17
eighteen
18
nineteen
19
twenty
20

Chapter 7

Morphology

> "Los idiomas están en constante evolución; con cada generación se transforman, al añadirse nuevas palabras, al dejarse de usar otras, al crearse expresiones o al dar un valor distinto a aquellas que ya existían. Las palabras se forman, se modifican, cambiando de significado y de uso".
>
> *"Languages are constantly evolving; with each generation they are transformed, as new words are added, others are dropped, expressions are created, or as different value is given to those that already existed. Words are formed and modified, as they change in meaning and usage."*
>
> –Ada & Campoy, 2020

In this chapter, we dive into the language subsystem of morphology and its role in cross-linguistic instruction. Morphology helps us understand the ways words are built by combining smaller units called morphemes. It is concerned with the rules and patterns governing the internal structure of words, and how these morphemes, which are the smallest units of meaning in a language, are combined to convey meaning. Understanding the rules and patterns governing the formation of words is essential when analyzing cross-linguistic Spanish-English relationships. Morphology provides the foundation for vocabulary development, spelling, decoding, word recognition, word formation, and reading comprehension. Developing morphological awareness is an important aspect of literacy and biliteracy instruction and significantly impacts students' reading and writing abilities across languages (Carlisle, 1995; Deacon & Kirby, 2004; Leonet et al., 2020).

In This Chapter

Morphology

Morphology is a branch of linguistics that examines the structure and formation of words in a language. In alphabetical languages such as Spanish and English, morphemes or word parts are combined to create different noun and verb forms, including variations in tense, aspect, plurality, and other grammatical features.

Both English and Spanish use inflectional morphology to convey grammatical information. **Inflectional morphology** refers to the addition of a morpheme that changes the meaning of that word. For example, with verbs, both languages use different endings to indicate tense, mood, aspect, and person. While the specific endings and rules vary between the languages, the concept of inflectional morphology is common to both. For example, in both Spanish and English, plurals can be formed by adding an **s** at the end of some nouns.

Derivational morphology refers to the process of forming new words by adding affixes (prefixes, suffixes) to a root or a base word. This process changes the grammatical category or meaning of the original word. Words created through derivational morphology are related, but they have different functions and meanings. For example, the derivatives of the word *action* (noun) maintain related meanings while the function (part of speech/grammatical category) of the word changes according to a given context in both English and Spanish.

Function	English	Spanish
noun	action	acción
verb	acting	actuando
adjective	active	activo
adverb	actively	activamente

Shared Morphologic Ancestry

English and Spanish are two languages with different linguistic origins and structures, so their morphologies are distinct in many ways. However, they do share some common elements and similarities due to their common Indo-European heritage and the influence of Latin on both languages. Let's explore how English and Spanish morphology are related and different.

> Both English and Spanish belong to the Indo-European language family, which means they share some common linguistic roots.

Both English and Spanish belong to the Indo-European language family, which means they share some common linguistic roots. Proto-Indo-European is the ancestral language that gave rise to both English and Spanish, among many other languages. The relationship between Spanish and English morphology stems from Latin and Greek.

Latin had a significant influence on both languages, albeit at different historical periods. Latin is the ancestor of the Romance languages, including Spanish, and it has had a direct influence on Spanish morphology. In English, Latin influence came primarily through Norman French after the Norman Conquest of England in the 11th century.

In the previous chapter, we took an in-depth look at orthography and its role in cross-linguistic instruction. While orthography is concerned with the visual representation of words in writing, morphology focuses on the internal structure and formation of those words. Understanding the interrelationship between morphology and orthography is crucial for a comprehensive understanding of a language's structure and usage as well as the cross-linguistic relationships that exist between Spanish and English.

Caveat

Despite their similarities, it's important to note that English and Spanish have distinct morphological systems due to their separate linguistic histories. The way they handle tense, aspect, mood, and other grammatical features can differ significantly. Additionally, the specific rules governing word formation and inflectional morphology can vary widely between the two languages.

Morphology and Biliteracy

Morphology is a crucial component of biliteracy. It plays a significant role in understanding and producing written language. Recall that morphology is the study of the structure and formation of words, including the identification, analysis, and description of the meaningful units (morphemes) that make up words. Morphemes are the smallest units of meaning in a language and can be words or parts of words, such as prefixes, suffixes, and roots.

Morphological knowledge helps individuals understand the meaning of words. By understanding prefixes, suffixes, and root words, readers can discern or decipher the meanings of unfamiliar words. For example, knowing that **un-** is a prefix meaning "not" can help a reader understand the meaning of words like *unhappy* or *unsuccessful*. Therefore, morphology supports comprehension and vocabulary development.

As previously discussed, there is an interrelationship between orthography (spelling) and morphology. In both Spanish and English, morphological awareness helps with encoding and decoding unfamiliar words. When readers are aware of common prefixes, suffixes, and root words, they can break down complex words into meaningful parts, making it easier to spell and read them. For example, knowing that **happi** is a root meaning "fortunate" and **-ness** is a suffix indicating a state or quality, a reader can understand the word *happiness* more easily.

Morphological awareness also helps students understand how words are formed by combining morphemes. This understanding helps in generating new words, understanding word relationships, and expanding vocabulary. For example, knowing that **act** is a root and **-ion** is a suffix forming a noun, one can understand the formation of the word *action*.

This morphological knowledge contributes to reading comprehension by enabling readers to grasp the nuances of word meanings within a given context. It allows readers to understand the subtleties of words and phrases, enhancing overall comprehension skills.

Cross-Linguistic Connections

Spanish and English are both Indo-European languages, but they belong to different branches within this language family. Spanish is a Romance language, descendant from Latin, while English is a Germanic language. Despite these differences, there are important cross-linguistic connections in morphology due to historical influences and shared linguistic features. For example, the root words borrowed from both the Latin and Greek languages expand through derivations to form multiple cognates. In addition, while the specifics of verb conjugation differ between Spanish and English, both languages mark verb forms to indicate tense, person, and number. In the next section, we will define more explicitly these cross-linguistic connections through inflectional and derivational morphology.

Key Terms

Inflected Language: Languages where the form of a word indicates grammatical features such as tense, mood, gender, number, and case.

Derivational Morphology: The process of forming new words by adding affixes (prefixes, suffixes) to a root or a base word.

Cognates: Words that have a similar meaning and similar spelling in different languages because they share a common origin.

Inflectional Morphology in Spanish and English

Spanish, like many other Romance languages, is considered a highly inflected language, meaning that changes in the form of words indicate grammatical features such as tense, mood, gender, number, and case. The inflectional nature of Spanish can be traced back to its Latin origins, as Spanish evolved from the Latin spoken on the Iberian Peninsula. This inflectional morphology is a legacy of Latin and is more preserved in Spanish compared to English.

Spanish uses inflections to convey various grammatical categories such as gender, number, and person. Nouns, adjectives, and articles change their forms to match the gender and number of the nouns they modify.

Spanish verbs are highly inflected, changing their forms to indicate tense, mood, aspect, person, and number. There are numerous conjugation patterns, and verbs can be conjugated differently based on the subject and the context.

Adjectives in Spanish must agree in gender and number with the nouns they modify. This requires inflections in the form of endings to match the characteristics of the noun.

Pronouns in Spanish also undergo inflections to indicate grammatical features such as person, gender, and number. The inflected forms of pronouns help convey specific meanings and roles in a sentence.

The inflectional nature of Spanish contributes to its expressive richness and precision in conveying thoughts and feelings.

Noun	Affix	Grammatical Feature
libro	-o	gender, masculine
libros	-s	plurality
librito	-ito	diminutive
librote	-ote	augmentative
librazo	-azo	aspect
librero	-ero	derivative

Verb	Affix	Grammatical Feature
escribir	-ir	infinitive form
escribiendo	-iendo	gerund or present progressive
escribo	-o	first person, simple present tense
escribí	-í	first person, simple past tense
escribiré	é	first person, future tense

English has lost much of its inflectional morphology over time. While it still retains some inflectional elements (e.g., plural **-s**, past-tense **-ed**), they are more limited compared to Spanish. The loss of inflectional affixes in English is a result of historical, linguistic, cultural, and social factors that have shaped the language over time. Several factors contributed to this linguistic evolution. Old English, the earliest form of English, was a highly inflected language, similar to modern German. However, over time, due to historical events such as the Norman Conquest in 1066, English underwent simplification and adopted elements from Norman French, contributing to the loss of inflections. English has developed a preference for analytic structures, where meaning is conveyed through word order, auxiliary verbs, and prepositions rather than inflectional endings.

Noun	Affix	Grammatical Feature
books	-s	plurality
booklet	-let	diminutive
bookshelf	-shelf	compound
booker	-er	derivative

Verb	Affix	Grammatical Feature
to walk	N/A	infinitive form
walking	-ing	gerund or present progressive
walks	-s	second person, simple present tense
walked	-ed	simple past tense

Learn More

Cenoz, J., & Santos, A. (2020). Implementing pedagogical translanguaging in trilingual schools. *System*, *92*, 1–9.

Marks, R. A., Sun, X., McAlister López, E., Nickerson, N., Hernández, I., Caruso, V. C., Satterfield, T., & Kovelman, I. (2022). Cross-linguistic differences in the associations between morphological awareness and reading in Spanish and English in young simultaneous bilinguals. *International Journal of Bilingual Education and Bilingualism, 25*(10), 3907–3923.

English and Spanish also share derivational affixes, which are prefixes or suffixes added to word roots to create new words or change their meaning. Prefixes, roots, and suffixes are morphemes that can sometimes stand alone as words or be compounded to form new words or word derivatives.

Key Terms

Derivational Affixes: Morphological units that convey meaning through prefixes, roots, and suffixes. Greek and Latin derivational affixes have a positive cross-linguistic transfer across languages.

Prefix: An affix that is placed before the stem of a word to create a new word. For example, the prefix **trans**- means "across."

Root: The stem part of the word to which prefixes and suffixes can be attached to create a new word. For example, the root **form** means "shape."

Suffix: An affix that is placed after the stem of a word to create a new word. For example, the suffix **-tion** means "action" or "process."

Cognates

Spanish-English cognates are words that have a similar meaning and similar spelling in both languages because they share a common origin, usually Latin or Greek. Due to historical and linguistic influences, many words in Spanish and English have parallel forms, which include the same morphological units of meaning across languages, making it easier for speakers of one language to recognize and understand words in the other. Cognates provide insights into the shared linguistic roots of these languages.

Prefix trans-	Root Form	Suffix -tion/-ción
transform *transforma*	*form* *forma*	*transformation* *transformación*

Cognates are important linguistic features that help develop cross-linguistic understanding, as well as metacognitive and metalinguistic skills. Cognates can significantly expand academic vocabulary across languages. Cognates also offer a bridge for learners to communicate more effectively in both languages.

However, it is crucial to be aware of some caveats associated with cognates.

- **False Cognates:** Not all words that look and sound similar in both languages have the same meaning. False cognates are words that may look alike but have different meanings. For example, the word *sympathy* in English does not mean *simpatía* in Spanish; the correct meaning and translation for *sympathy* in Spanish is *compasión*.
- **Pronunciation Differences:** While the spelling of cognates may be similar, the pronunciations may differ. It is essential to pay attention to pronunciation and accents to avoid confusion.
- **Word Usage and Connotations:** Even when the meanings are similar, there might be subtle differences in how cognates are used or the connotations they carry. Understanding these nuances is important for accurate communication.

In other words, Spanish-English cognates can be a valuable tool for language learners, providing a shortcut to understanding and expanding vocabulary. However, learners should be cautious of false cognates and be aware of pronunciation and usage differences to apply them effectively.

In Action

What follows are four sample lessons that address the bidirectional dynamics of inflectional morphology and derivational morphology. The first two lessons are correlated to first-grade foundational skill standards and focus on inflectional morphology. The Spanish to English lesson will review formation of plurals by adding -s and -es in Spanish and compare this to the pluralization adding an -s in English. The English to Spanish lesson expands on pluralization by contrasting the use of -es to form plurals. The third and fourth lessons are correlated to word study in Grades 3–5. These lessons focus on derivational morphology where students explore suffixes and how they impact word function and meaning.

Spanish to English Lesson: Inflections to Form Plurals (Grade 1)

In Unit 1 of Grade 1, the concept of nouns is introduced, followed by the pluralization of nouns. Mrs. Gómez and Mrs. Johnson plan lessons to convey pluralization by adding -s or -es at the end of nouns. Students learn that in Spanish as well as in English, a plural is formed by adding the affix -s or -es at the end of a noun. However, there are different rules in Spanish and English that govern when to add -s or -es to form a plural.

Paso 1: Usar lo que ya sabemos y hemos aprendido sobre el español

<table>
<tr>
<td>Establecer el objetivo de la lección y la relación de transferencia

Repasar la función gramatical de los nombres y la pluralización en español

Confirmar la formación del plural añadiendo -s cuando el sustantivo termina en vocal y -es cuando termina en consonante</td>
<td>Hoy vamos a comparar y contrastar <u>una</u> de las maneras de formar los plurales en español y en inglés. Descubriremos que es parecido, pero no exactamente igual.
Muestre un cartel que clasifica sustantivos por sus categorías.
Recuerden que los sustantivos son palabras que representan los nombres que le damos a las personas, lugares, animales y cosas.
Escriba la palabra libro.
¿Qué palabra usamos si queremos decir más de un libro?
(Estudiantes: Libros)
Correcto: Libros.
Añada -s para indicar el plural de la palabra libro.
En español, cuando queremos indicar más de una persona, lugar, animal o cosa le añadimos una -s al final de las palabras cuando terminan en vocal. Pero miren bien aquí: cuando el sustantivo termina en consonante, le añadimos -es.</td>
<td>
<table>
<tr><td>libro</td><td></td></tr>
<tr><td>libros</td><td></td></tr>
<tr><td>árbol</td><td></td></tr>
<tr><td>árboles</td><td></td></tr>
</table>
</td>
</tr>
<tr>
<td>Mostrar como añadir -s o -es a sustantivos para indicar el plural</td>
<td>Muestre la lista de palabras en español.
Vamos a repasar como formar el plural de estas palabras juntos.
Señale cada palabra y pregunte:
La palabra es _______.
¿Termina en vocal o consonante?
¿Añadimos -s o -es al final para formar el plural?
¿Cómo se dice más de un o una ______?
Correcto: se dice ___________.</td>
<td>
<table>
<tr><th>Singular</th><th>Plural</th></tr>
<tr><td>mesa</td><td>mesa___</td></tr>
<tr><td>oso</td><td>oso___</td></tr>
<tr><td>reloj</td><td>reloj___</td></tr>
<tr><td>animal</td><td>animal___</td></tr>
<tr><td>león</td><td>leon___</td></tr>
<tr><td>doctor</td><td>doctor___</td></tr>
<tr><td></td><td></td></tr>
</table>
</td>
</tr>
</table>

Paso 2: Conectar, comparar y contrastar con el inglés

Preparación de manipulativos

Colaboración y trabajo en pares o grupos

Promover conocimientos previos y asociaciones

Invitar a los estudiantes a compartir conocimientos con un compañero

Afirmar la comparación y contraste entre ambos idiomas

Prepare imágenes y tarjetas de pares de sustantivos en español y en inglés para cada grupo de estudiantes.

Ahora ustedes van a formar los plurales de los sustantivos en inglés.

Primero pida a los estudiantes que organicen el par de sustantivos en inglés y en español con la imagen que les corresponde.

Luego pida que piensen y digan el plural de los sustantivos en inglés.

Usen las imágenes para organizar los pares de palabras en inglés y en español.

Haga las siguientes preguntas mientras señala cada palabra y añade la -s para indicar el plural en inglés.

¿Cómo se dice perro en inglés?
¿Cómo se dice más de un perro en inglés?
¿Qué tenemos que añadir al final de la palabra? ___

En pares o grupos pequeños invite a los estudiantes a correlacionar las palabras y añadir una -s para formar el plural en inglés.

Opciones colaborativas:

1. Muestre una tabla de imágenes y tarjetas de palabras de sustantivos que incluyan algunos de los que ya se repasaron en español.
2. Reproduzca la tabla de imágenes, sustantivos y actividades para cada par de estudiantes.

Para formar el plural en español se añade un -s al final de palabras que terminan con vocal y se añade -es a palabras que terminan en consonante. Para formar el plural de muchas palabras en inglés solo se añade una -s al final de muchas de las palabras no importa si terminan en vocal o en consonante.

Español Singular	Foto	Inglés Singular	Inglés Plural
perro		dog	dog___
gato		cat	cat___
serpiente		snake	snake___
hormiga		ant	ant___
oso		bear	bear___
banana		banana	banana__
animal		animal	animal___
doctor		doctor	doctor___
reloj		clock	clock___

<table>
<tr><th colspan="3">Paso 3: Promover destrezas metalingüísticas al resumir lo aprendido</th></tr>
<tr><td>Resumir lo aprendido</td><td>Muestre el organizador gráfico para resumir lo aprendido sobre la pluralización en español y en inglés.

Pida a pares de estudiantes que expliquen lo que aprendieron.

¿Qué hemos aprendido sobre formar el plural en español y en inglés?</td><td><table><tr><th>Español</th><th>Ambos</th><th>Inglés</th></tr><tr><td>Cuando terminan en vocal se añade -s

Cuando terminan en consonante se añade -es</td><td>Los sustantivos pueden ser singular (uno solo) o plural (más de uno)</td><td>Se añade -s cuando terminan en vocal o consonante</td></tr></table></td></tr>
<tr><td>Afirmar la lectoescritura bilingüe y las conexiones con el inglés</td><td colspan="2">Ya aprendieron una de las maneras para formar el plural tanto en español como en inglés. Otro día vamos a aprender otras formas de formar el plural de palabras en español y en inglés.</td></tr>
</table>

Morphology is a crucial component of biliteracy.

English to Spanish Lesson: Inflections to Form Plurals (Grade 1)

Mrs. Johnson and Mrs. Gómez will continue exploring pluralization of nouns with their Grade 1 students in the coming units. Mrs. Johnson will build on the Spanish to English bridging lesson by comparing and contrasting the second pluralization rule in English: adding **-es** when the nouns end in **-s**,**-ss**, **-z**, **-x**, **-ch** and **-sh**.

<table>
<tr><th colspan="3">Step 1: Review what we know and have learned about English</th></tr>
<tr>
<td>State Lesson Objective

Review Concepts Already Learned About English</td>
<td>Today we are going to learn another way to show more than one in English. Then we will explore how it may be the same or different in Spanish.

Remind students what they already know about pluralization.

Singular means "one."
Plural means "more than one."
We have already learned that we make a singular noun plural by adding an -s at the end of the word. Let's review by forming the plural of these words.

Display the list of words. Point to each one, ask the question below, then add the -s.

How do you say more than one _____?</td>
<td><table>
<tr><th>Singular</th><th>Plural</th></tr>
<tr><td>boat</td><td>boat___</td></tr>
<tr><td>car</td><td>car___</td></tr>
<tr><td>bike</td><td>bike___</td></tr>
<tr><td>truck</td><td>truck___</td></tr>
<tr><td>train</td><td>train___</td></tr>
<tr><td>wagon</td><td>wagon___</td></tr>
<tr><td>plane</td><td>plane___</td></tr>
<tr><td>ship</td><td>ship___</td></tr>
</table></td>
</tr>
<tr>
<td>Model Adding -es to Nouns Ending in s, ss, x, z, ch, sh</td>
<td>Show nouns that end in s, ss, x, z, ch, sh. Ask: What happens when a word already ends with an s?

How do we show that we mean more than one when the word ends with an s or letters that make or are similar to the /s/ sound?

In English, we add -es when a word ends in s or in consonants -s, -ss, -z, -x, or in consonant digraphs ch and sh.</td>
<td><table>
<tr><th>Singular</th><th>Plural</th></tr>
<tr><td>bus</td><td>bus___</td></tr>
<tr><td>dress</td><td>dress___</td></tr>
<tr><td>box</td><td>box___</td></tr>
<tr><td>couch</td><td>couch___</td></tr>
<tr><td>dish</td><td>dish___</td></tr>
</table></td>
</tr>
</table>

Step 2: Connect, compare, and contrast to Spanish

Collaboration (Pairs or Small Groups)

Promote Prior Knowledge and Use of All Linguistic Resources

Model

Invite Students to Share What They Have Learned with a Partner

Compare and Contrast English and Spanish

Next students will work in pairs to add -es to create plural nouns in English. Review the list of words.

Ask students to say the word in Spanish. Discuss meaning of words or ask students to turn to their partners and use the words in a simple sentence to ensure comprehension.

How do you say more than one bus? What do we need to add to the word _____ to make it plural?

We add -es

Next, you will work in pairs to add -es to form plural nouns in English.

Remember, in English we add -es when a noun ends in consonants.

In Spanish we add -es when nouns end in with a consonant.

Singular	Plural
bus	bus___
dress	dress___
boss	boss___
glass	glass___
wax	wax___
box	box___
fox	fox___
mix	mix___
buzz	buzz___
couch	couch___
peach	peach___
fish	fish___
wish	wish___
dish	dish___
bush	bush___

Step 3: Promote metalinguistic skills by summarizing what was learned

Summarize What Was Learned

Display an anchor chart to show pluralization using -es in English and in Spanish. Ask students to discuss with a partner what they learned about forming plurals in English and in Spanish by adding -es at the end of some nouns.

Notice that consonants s, ss, sh, x, z, and ch represent sounds that are similar to the /s/ sound. That is why in English we add -es so we can clearly communicate more than one.

English	Both	Spanish
Add -s for most nouns whether ending in vowels or consonants—EXCEPT, add -es when the noun ends in s, ss, sh, x, z, and ch.	Nouns can be singular (only one) or plural (more than one).	Add-s when the noun ends in a vowel. Add -es When the noun ends in a consonant.

Affirm Biliteracy and Language Connections

Now you have learned some of the rules about forming plural words in English and in Spanish.
Adding -es to form a plural in English and Spanish helps you pronounce certain words better in each language.

Spanish to English Lesson: Derivational Affixes (Grade 4)

Mr. Cuevas and Mrs. Harrison are fourth-grade teachers planning the cross-linguistic transfer opportunities for their unit on Earth Changes. They analyze the text and notice that many of the content words contain Greek and Latin suffixes. They plan to use the content words in the text relating to Earth Changes to prepare a cross-linguistic transfer lesson focusing on derivational affixes (prefixes, roots, and affixes). Mr. Cuevas will conduct a bridging lesson on the suffix **-cion** and its correlation to the suffix **-tion** in English. Students will explore the word derivatives in Spanish and English.

Paso 1: Usar lo que ya sabemos y hemos aprendido en español

Establecer el objetivo

Repasar lo que es un sufijo

Establecer la relación de transferencia

Reconocer y definir palabras que contienen el sufijo **-ción**

Promover conocimientos previos y asociaciones

Hoy vamos a repasar los sufijos en español y explorar cómo funcionan los sufijos tanto en español como en inglés.
Cuando estudiamos palabras, generalmente estudiamos sus partes. Un sufijo es la parte de la palabra que se añade al final después de la raíz.

Un sufijo tiene su propio significado. Cuando le añadimos un sufijo a una palabra, cambiamos el significado o función de la palabra en una oración. Muchos prefijos en español y en inglés provienen del idioma latín y del griego.

Vamos a repasar palabras con el sufijo -ción. El sufijo -ción cambia un verbo a un sustantivo.
El sufijo -ción quiere decir "el proceso de, o la acción de".
El sufijo -ción en algunas palabras también se escribe -sión; -xión y -cción.
Muestre un cartel para repasar el significado del sufijo -ción y proveer varios ejemplos.

El verbo es: _(observar)__
Le añadimos el sufijo -ción
*Ahora dice: _(observación)_*
Significa la acción o proceso de (observar).

verbo	sustantivo
observar	observación
elevar	elevación
informar	información
formar	formación
sedimentar	sedimentación
desintegrar	desintegración
erupcionar	erupción
meteorizar	meteorización
radiar	radiación
oxidar	oxidación

Verb	Noun
observe	observation
elevate	elevation
inform	information
form	formation
sediment	sedimentation
disintegrate	disintegration
erupt	eruption
radiate	radiation
oxidate	oxidation

Paso 2: Conectar, comparar y contrastar con el inglés

Establecer conexión entre los idiomas

Promover conocimientos previos y asociaciones

Invite a los estudiantes a compartir conocimientos con un compañero

¿Qué notan de estas palabras? ¿Cómo se les dice a las palabras que quieren decir lo mismo y se escriben casi igual en dos idiomas? (cognados)

Una excepción en la lista es: meteorización que en inglés se dice weathering.

Estas palabras son cognados porque comparten el mismo sufijo que proviene del latín.

El sufijo -ción es equivalente al sufijo --tion en inglés.

Ahora ustedes van a trabajar en pares para completar la tabla de palabras con los sufijos -ción en español al inglés.

Después trabajarán juntos para completar la tabla de verbos en en inglés y en español.

¿Qué notaron sobre todas estas palabras?

Todas estas palabras son cognados porque provienen del latín, que es un idioma base para el español y que influye en muchas palabras del inglés.

Español	Inglés
adaptación	
creación	
celebración	
educación	
exploración	
extinción	
liberación	
presentación	
producción	
investigación	
meteorización	

Inglés	Español
adapt	
	crear
celebrate	
	educar
explore	
	liberar
present	
	producir
investigate	

<table>
<tr><th colspan="3">Paso 3: Promover destrezas metalingüísticas al resumir lo aprendido</th></tr>
<tr><td>Resumir lo aprendido</td><td>¿Qué hemos aprendido hoy?
Hemos aprendido que muchas de las palabras que comparten el mismo sufijo en español y en inglés son cognados. Los cognados son palabras en dos idiomas distintos (como el español y el inglés) que provienen de una misma lengua (como el latín). Los cognados se escriben casi igual en dos idiomas y tienen el mismo significado.</td><td><table><tr><th>Español</th><th>Ambos</th><th>Inglés</th></tr><tr><td>El sufijo
-ción
-sión
-xión
-cción</td><td>Proviene del latín y quiere decir acción o proceso.</td><td>El sufijo
-tion
-sion</td></tr></table></td></tr>
<tr><td>Afirmar la lectoescritura bilingüe y las conexiones entre los idiomas</td><td colspan="2">Es importante estudiar las partes de las palabras como los prefijos, raíces y prefijos. Muchos de estos morfemas, o partes de palabras, provienen del latín y del griego y por lo tanto forman cognados entre el español y el inglés. ¡Esto multiplica el vocabulario de un estudiante bilingüe!</td></tr>
</table>

English to Spanish Lesson: Derivational Affixes (Grade 4)

During the English bridging time, Ms. Harrison reminds the students that they have already studied the English suffix **-tion** (as in *creation*) and the Spanish suffix **-ción** (as in *creación*) both serve the purpose of forming nouns from verbs. She will now explain several equivalent English-Spanish cognate relationships using suffixes.

Step 1: Review what we know and have learned in English		
State Lesson Objective Review Concepts Already Learned About English Model Affirm the Cross-Linguistic Connection	*Today we are going to learn about suffixes that are equivalent in English and Spanish.* *Remember that suffixes are word parts attached to the root of a word. Suffixes change the meaning and function of the base word or root word. We already know about suffixes like -tion and -ción. When added to a verb, the word becomes a noun.* *The suffix -ate is equivalent to the suffix -ar. In both English and Spanish, they signal an action word or verb.* Display the English/Spanish list of words. Point to each word as you use the "I say-You say" strategy. Teachers say the English word, and students call out the Spanish word. *When I say: duplicate, you say duplicar.* Repeat with each cognate listed. *All these words are cognates and have the same function: they are verbs. They signal an action.*	(see word list below)

English	Spanish
Suffix -ate	Suffix -ar
I say:	*You say:*
duplicate	duplicar
evaluate	evaluar
facilitate	facilitar
illustrate	ilustrar
locate	localizar
narrate	narrar
formulate	formular
participate	participar
demonstrate	demostrar
accelerate	acelerar

Step 2: Connect, compare, and contrast to Spanish

Collaboration (Pairs or Small Groups)

Invite Students to Share What They Have Learned with a Partner

Additional Collaboration Activity

Now it is your turn to work with your partner to pair English and Spanish words that have equivalent suffixes.

Invite partners to read the list together using the "I say-You say" strategy.

Let students know that there are other suffixes that signal word function or part of speech.

Motivate students to generate a list of cognates with equivalent suffixes.

Function	English	Spanish
adjectives	academ**ic** bas**ic**	acadé**mico** bás**ico**
	fam**ous** curi**ous** fabul**ous**	fam**oso** curi**oso** fabul**oso**

English	Spanish
Abstract Nouns	Sustantivos Abstractos
Suffix -ence	Suffix -encia
I say:	*You say:*
intelligence	inteligencia
existence	existencia
essence	esencia
patience	paciencia
science	ciencia
consequence	consecuencia
difference	diferencia

English	Spanish
Adverbs	Adverbios
Suffix -ly	Suffix -mente
I say:	*You say:*
correctly	correctamente
directly	directamente
perfectly	perfectamente
completely	completamente
fortunately	afortunadamente
naturally	naturalmente
totally	totalmente

Step 3: Promote metalinguistic skills by summarizing what was learned

Summarize What Was Learned

In both English and Spanish suffixes:

- *are added to the root of a word,*
- *signal the function or part of speech,*
- *are usually cognates.*

English	Both	Spanish
suffixes	▪ added to the root word ▪ signal the function of the word ▪ are cognates	los sufijos

Affirm Biliteracy Cross-Linguistic Connections

Word parts like prefixes, roots, and suffixes help you recognize the meaning of words. English and Spanish cognates share word parts. Recognizing the meaning of a cognate in one language will help you understand its meaning in the other language.

Assessment Considerations

In both Spanish and English, assessing students' morphological knowledge involves evaluating their understanding of the structure and formation of words, including prefixes, suffixes, roots, and other morphemes. The emphasis of the assessment in a cross-linguistic context relates to how meaning can be discerned across languages.

Here are some methods and formative strategies that can be used to assess students' morphological knowledge in a bilingual context:

- Focus on words that include Greek or Latin prefixes and suffixes in one language and ask students to provide the word in the other language.
- Give students a list of words in one language. Ask them to use a derivational suffix to change the grammatical function of the word, then use the new word in a sentence in the partner language.
- Provide students with a list of suffixes in one language and have them generate words in that language and their equivalent cognates in the other.
- Give students a few sentences where they need to infer the meaning of words based on their morphological structure. Have students translate the sentence into the other language.
- Have students use roots, prefixes, and suffixes to create a brand-new term that can be used across languages and applied to describe an idea, object, or process.

Pause and Reflect

How does morphological knowledge contribute to reading comprehension?

What are some cognates you should review with your students?

Conclusion

The study of morphology involves the analysis of how words are formed and modified, with an emphasis on morphemes as the smallest units of meaning in a language. The comparison of English and Spanish morphologies reveals both shared elements and distinct features, highlighting their common Indo-European heritage and the influence of Latin and Greek languages.

This chapter has underscored the crucial link between morphology and orthography, emphasizing the significance of understanding both the internal structure and visual representation of words in writing. Morphology is positioned as a foundational aspect of language skills, playing a vital role in vocabulary development, spelling, decoding, word recognition, word formation, and reading comprehension.

Inflectional morphology sheds light on the contrasting features of Spanish and English. While Spanish retains a highly inflected nature, especially in verbs, English has experienced a reduction in inflectional elements, favoring analytic structures.

Derivational morphology, focusing on the formation of new words through affixes, reveals a shared ancestry in Latin and Greek by English and Spanish. The resulting cognates contribute to the extensive similarities in spelling and meanings between the two languages. The teaching of derivational suffixes highlights their importance in changing the grammatical category or function of words, facilitating vocabulary expansion and nuanced expression for bilingual speakers and writers.

Key Takeaways

Morphology involves the study of how words are formed and modified, emphasizing the role of morphemes—the smallest units of meaning in a language.

English and Spanish, though distinct in their linguistic origins, share common elements due to their Indo-European heritage and the influence of the Latin and Greek languages.

Morphology is essential for the development of various language skills, including vocabulary development, spelling, decoding, word recognition, word formation, and reading comprehension.

In both English and Spanish, inflectional suffixes change the meaning of a word, but do not change the grammatical function of a word.

In both English and Spanish, derivational suffixes change the meaning and grammatical function of words.

English and Spanish share derivational affixes rooted in Latin and Greek, resulting in cognates—words with similar spelling and meanings in both languages.

Chapter 8

Semantics

"Las palabras son velas que iluminan el camino hacia la verdad. Como cada palabra tiene un alma, hay en cada verso, además de la armonía verbal, una melodía ideal".

"Words are candles that light the way to the truth. Because each word has a soul, there is in each verse, in addition to verbal harmony, an ideal melody."

—Rubén Darío as cited in Machado, 2022

This chapter delves into the significance of semantics in teaching and learning vocabulary. Vocabulary can be defined as the set of words known or used by an individual, while word knowledge encompasses understanding, familiarity, and usage of words. Semantics focuses on the relationships between words and the meaning they convey. This chapter underscores the importance of word relationships, grasping contextual nuances, recognizing word families, mastering word usage, honing precision, and developing conceptual understandings.

While conceptual knowledge can transfer easily, word knowledge needs explicit instruction. To this end, this chapter addresses practical strategies for cross-linguistic transfer of semantic constructs such as vocabulary, word relationships, and word form and functions.

The concept of equivalency is also explored, emphasizing the importance of understanding it for effective communication and translation between languages. Equivalence involves understanding word meanings, nuances, and appropriate usage in various contexts.

In This Chapter

Semantics

Semantics is the study of word meanings in language. Essentially, semantics explores the relationships between words and the meanings they represent, for example, antonyms, synonyms, cognates, or levels of specificity. It involves the analysis and understanding of how words, phrases, and sentences convey meaning, both in isolation and within the context of a particular language. Semantics is highly interrelated to vocabulary and word knowledge.

Words simply refer to individual units of language that have meaning and can stand alone or be combined to form phrases and sentences. Vocabulary, on the other hand, encompasses the entire set of words a person knows or uses in a particular language. Importantly, a rich vocabulary allows individuals to express themselves more precisely and understand others better. While vocabulary is part of semantics, semantics also involves the study of meaning structures and how words relate to each other in conveying meaning. A deep understanding of vocabulary and semantics supports language comprehension and communication.

Key Terms

Vocabulary: A component of semantics, vocabulary refers to the set of words that a person knows or uses in a particular language or field of knowledge.

Word Recognition: The process of identifying written words quickly and with accuracy.

Word Knowledge: A person's understanding and familiarity with words, including their meanings, usage, and pronunciation. It encompasses vocabulary and the ability to comprehend, use, and interpret words in various contexts.

To clarify further, semantics is the broader study of meaning in language, while vocabulary specifically refers to the words known or used by an individual to express knowledge in a language. As such, words are the building blocks of language that have meaning and represent objects, actions, emotions, and concepts. In the context of vocabulary acquisition, understanding semantics involves grasping the meanings of words, their nuances, and how they interact within a language.

Here are some ways that semantics relates to teaching and learning vocabulary and word knowledge.

Word Relationships	Semantics helps learners establish connections between words and their meanings. Understanding the semantic relationships between words aids in retaining and recalling vocabulary more effectively.
Contextual Understanding	Semantics helps learners comprehend words within different contexts. Teaching vocabulary in context allows students to understand how words are used in sentences and how their meanings can vary based on the context.
Word Families	Semantics helps learners recognize word families and derivations. Understanding the roots, prefixes, and suffixes of words can contribute to a more profound comprehension of vocabulary, making it easier for learners to infer the meanings of unfamiliar words.
Word Usage and Precision	Semantics helps learners choose words with precision. Understanding the subtle differences in meaning between closely related words allows individuals to express themselves more precisely and accurately.
Conceptual Understanding	Semantics goes beyond individual words to encompass the understanding of ideas and relationships between concepts. Teaching vocabulary in a way that emphasizes the underlying concepts helps learners develop a broader understanding of the language.

Semantics is a language subsystem that is fundamental to the effective teaching and learning of vocabulary. It involves not only knowing words but also understanding their meanings, relationships, and usage within a broader linguistic context. Semantics is intricately connected to the other language subsystems because understanding word meaning also involves consideration of syntax, morphology, phonology, and pragmatics.

Semantics and Biliteracy

Semantics is integral to language development. As learners acquire more words and understand their meanings, they become more proficient in expressing themselves and comprehending others. Strong semantic skills in one language can facilitate the transfer of skills to another language. Understanding the semantic relationships between words in different languages helps learners make connections and achieve proficiency in both languages. When students know the meaning of words and how words relate to one another in one language, it helps them understand the meaning of words and the word relationships in a new language. It is essential that vocabulary and word knowledge are taught explicitly for biliteracy; while conceptual knowledge is easily transferable, it cannot be assumed that students will transfer word knowledge from one language to another.

In both Spanish and English, vocabulary knowledge and comprehension are intrinsically connected. If a reader does not know a sufficient percentage of the words in a text, comprehension is impossible. In fact, a reader's general vocabulary knowledge is the most effective predictor of how well that reader will be able to comprehend a text (Baumann & Kame'enui, 2003; Irvin, 1990; Yopp & Yopp, 2007). In biliteracy, reading comprehension relies heavily on semantics. Proficient semantic skills allow readers to understand the meaning of texts, infer information, and make connections between different parts of a text, fostering overall literacy development. As students acquire vocabulary, they can express themselves more precisely and comprehend a broader range of ideas. This is essential for both language acquisition and biliteracy.

While students can learn a great deal of vocabulary indirectly as they engage in oral language, listen to adults read aloud, or read on their own in each language, direct instruction of vocabulary and semantics for cross-linguistic transfer across languages is essential and accelerates biliteracy.

Cross-Linguistic Connections

In Chapter 7, I explained that cross-linguistic vocabulary connections between Spanish and English are often the result of historical and linguistic influences. Many words in both languages share a common origin, often tracing back to the Latin and Greek languages. For example:

Origin	Word	Meaning	Spanish Term	English Term
Greek	dēmokratíā	rule by the people	democracia	democracy
Latin	dictiōnārius	collection of words	diccionario	dictionary

In this chapter, we consider the equivalency of concept and vocabulary in cross-linguistic contexts. Equivalency of concept and vocabulary refers to the idea that different languages may have words or terms that represent the same or similar concepts. Finding equivalent expressions or terms for the same concept is certainly not a simple task, but learning equivalencies is essential for effective communication and translation between languages.

Key Terms

Equivalency: Being equal in value, significance, or meaning. When two things are considered equivalent, they are not just the same, they are interchangeable in a specific context.

Word Relationships: The connections or associations between words based on various linguistic and semantic aspects.

Caveat

Both Spanish and English boast a rich linguistic diversity that has evolved over centuries, influenced by historical, cultural, geographical, and modern global influences.

In an asset-oriented biliteracy program, the linguistic variations for terms and phrases are viewed as enriching and explored as dialects, regional variations, or distinct formal and informal registers. Students' linguistic variations are acknowledged, explored, and celebrated!

At a basic level, choosing an equivalent word seems straightforward because simple concepts usually have an equivalent term in another language. Some examples include: colors, shapes, numbers, sizes, objects (things), and academic terms.

Color		Color
rojo		red
amarillo		yellow
azul		blue

Objeto		Object
silla		chair
mesa		table
lámpara		lamp

Término académico		Academic Term
secuencia	1-2-3-4	sequence
comparar y contrastar		compare and contrast
causa y efecto	cause > effect	cause and effect

Equivalencies also depend on cultural nuances and connotations of words, however. Language learners, especially those aiming for biliteracy, need to understand the cultural context to use language appropriately and appreciate the subtleties of communication. Some concepts may not have a direct equivalency in the other language and translation may involve conveying the closest possible meaning rather than an exact match. This makes choosing the correct (or most appropriate) word or phrase to represent a concept more complicated.

Achieving vocabulary equivalency is sometimes challenging due to these cultural and linguistic differences. For example, consider these expressions:

Expresión	Meaning	Expression
"Te veré a las tres y cuarto."	The meaning is the same, but the way they are expressed differs.	"I will meet you at a quarter past three."
"¡Es pan comido!"	The intended meaning is the same, but the expression itself does not translate word-for-word.	"It's a piece of cake!"

> Understanding vocabulary equivalency is crucial for accurately conveying ideas and ensuring that the intended meaning is preserved across different languages.

In cross-linguistic studies or translation work, understanding vocabulary equivalency is crucial for accurately conveying ideas and ensuring that the intended meaning is preserved across different languages. It involves not only linguistic considerations but also considering cultural nuances and context to capture the richness of the original concept in the target language.

Semantics and vocabulary are foundational to language acquisition and biliteracy, as they underpin:

- effective communication
- vocabulary development
- cognitive abilities
- reading comprehension
- writing proficiency
- cultural understanding
- academic success in multiple languages

Cross-linguistic transfer lessons for vocabulary usually entail comparing the equivalent word relationships then contrasting the oral and written form of each term. Interactive, hands-on activities encourage students to manipulate visuals. Items such as as word cards are used to label concepts in both languages.

Manipulatives facilitate effective cross-linguistic vocabulary lessons.

Learn More

Yopp, R. H., & Yopp, H. K. (2007). Ten important words plus: A strategy for building word knowledge. *The Reading Teacher, 61*(2), 157–160.

Relyea, J. E., & Amendum, S. J. (2020). English reading growth in Spanish-speaking bilingual students: Moderating effect of English proficiency on cross-linguistic influence. *Child Development, 91*(4), 1150–1165.

Word Relationships

Word relationships refer to the connections or associations between words based on various linguistic and semantic aspects. Word relationships are constructs or concepts that exist equivalently in English and Spanish. In other words, the same word relationships exist in both languages, however, the terms or words are different and specific to each language. Word relationships can be categorized into different types, which are important for vocabulary knowledge and crucial for language comprehension. The comparison table shows equivalent word relationships in Spanish and English.

Understanding word relationships helps learners expand their vocabularies and improve their reading comprehension. Words provide context clues and readers can infer meanings, predict outcomes, and draw connections between ideas when they consider the subtle nuances in meanings and connotations.

Recognizing word relationship equivalency across languages is very beneficial for language learners as it contributes to their overall language proficiency, critical thinking, and effective oral and written communication.

> “Understanding word relationships helps learners expand their vocabularies and improve their reading comprehension.”

English	Spanish
Antonyms: words with opposite meanings (big-little; cold-hot; up-down)	**Antónimos:** palabras que expresan lo opuesto (grande-pequeño; frío-calor; arriba-abajo)
Synonyms: words with similar meanings (happy, joyful)	**Sinónimos:** palabras que tienen un significado parecido (contento, alegre)
Multiple Meanings: words that have more than one meaning (play, draw, drop)	**Significados múltiples:** palabras que tienen más de un significado (pata, hoja, saco)
Shades of Meaning: words that express degrees of a concept or quality (like, love, adore)	**Grados de significados:** grupo de palabras que expresan grados de un mismo concepto (querer, amar, adorar)
Levels of Specificity: words that describe at different levels of precision (living things, animal, mammal, domestic, cat)	**Niveles de especificación:** grupo de palabras que describen niveles o categorías de un mismo concepto (ser viviente, animal, mamífero, doméstico, gato)
Analogies: pairs of words that have the same relationship (___ is to ___ as ___ is to ___.) (Fork is to rake as spoon is to shovel.)	**Analogías:** dos palabras que tienen la misma relación (___ es a ___ como ___ es a ___.) (tenedor es a rastrillo como cuchara es a pala.)
Compound Words: words comprising two or more words (mailman, cowboy)	**Palabras compuestas:** palabras que se componen de otras dos palabras (sacapuntas, paraguas)
Homographs: words that are spelled the same but have different meanings (saw, play, like)	**Homógrafos:** palabras que se escriben iguales, pero tienen significados diferentes (como, gato, pata)
Homophones: words that sound the same but have different spellings and meanings (sea-see; write-right)	**Homófonos:** palabras que suenan iguales, pero se escriben diferente y tienen significados diferentes (bienes-vienes; Maya-malla; bota-vota)
Base Word Families: words that that have the same base word and related meaning (paint, painter, painting, painted)	**Palabras relacionadas:** palabras que tienen la misma palabra base y se relacionan por su significado (pinta, pintor, pintura, pintaba)
Cognates: words that are related through the same origin; they have the same meaning and are spelled almost the same in two different languages **English** / **Spanish** president / presidente institute / instituto artist / artista grace / gracia education / educación	**Cognados:** palabras que se relacionan por origen morfológico; estas palabras tienen el mismo significado y se deletrean casi igual en dos idiomas diferente. **español** / **inglés** presidente / president instituto / institute artista / artist gracia / grace educación / education

Vocabulary Strategies

Because of the equivalency at the word level and word relationship constructs between English and Spanish, cross-linguistic instruction of vocabulary is straightforward, fun, and effective. The use of simple manipulatives such as anchor charts, graphic organizers, vocabulary cards, pocket charts, and visuals is highly recommended. Students can work in pairs or small groups to negotiate meaning and match terms as they construct charts and use manipulatives. Teachers will often designate a bulletin board to cross-linguistic vocabulary study. Used during bridging time, these vocabulary strategies are easy to implement, interactive, and fundamental to conceptual development. Keep in mind that affirming and pointing out the equivalency of terms and concepts across languages is very important. Students make linguistic, cognitive, and cultural connections as they discuss their insights and compare and contrast terms.

When displaying cross-linguistic visuals and anchor charts, be sure to

- color code each language in some way,
- show academic language in both languages, and
- use a title that articulates the language construct or learning.

Bilingual Picture Vocabulary Logs

A vocabulary log can act as a point of reference for students as they acquire domain-specific vocabulary. In this example, the vocabulary associated with the life cycle of the frog is documented in both English and Spanish. As students gain more and more knowledge about frogs, they can reference the log to use vocabulary appropriately in each language.

Español		English
renacuajo		tadpole
huevo		egg
patas		legs
cola		tail
rana		frog

Interactive Classification Chart

This type of chart helps students classify vocabulary into different categories across languages. This visualizing of concepts helps students learn subject-specific vocabulary—in this case, nouns. Students can also practice speaking the words for each picture out loud in both languages.

niña	animal	lugar	planta	tronco
girl	animal	place	plant	log

Academic Language Interactive Pocket Chart

Interactive pocket charts can also support the acquisition of academic vocabulary. This chart about question words shows word equivalencies in English and Spanish. A manipulative chart like this is fun and engaging for students!

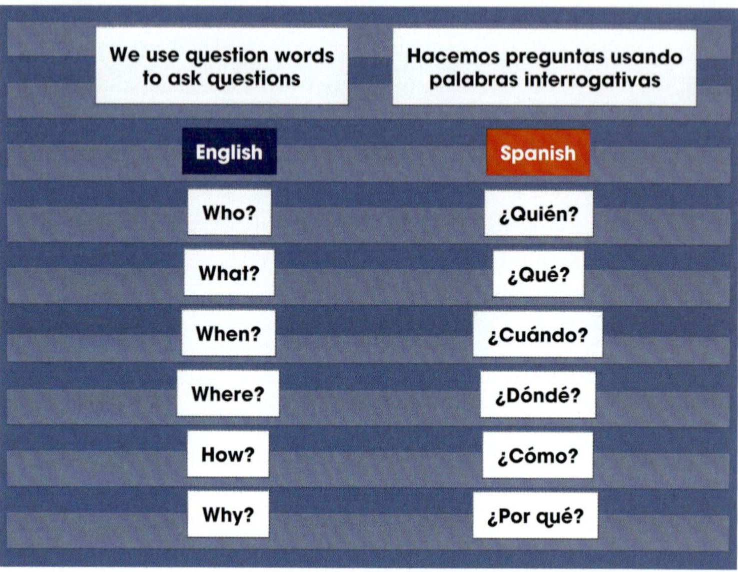

Process Posters with Bilingual Labels

Process posters with bilingual labels are another way to learn vocabulary and concept equivalencies. In this example, students labeled the process of photosynthesis. Seeing words side-by-side helps students recognize the content terms across languages. This type of chart also invites students to explain processes orally in each language.

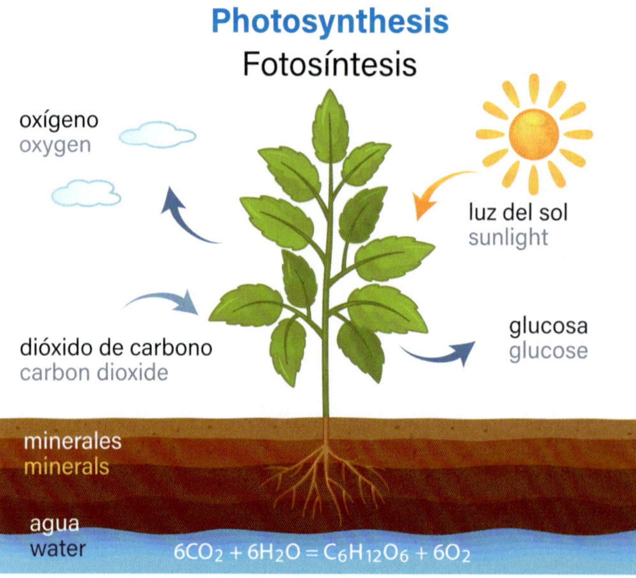

Cognate and Word Study Chart

Cognates can significantly expand academic vocabulary across languages. In this example, students make connections between English and Spanish words that share the Latin root **forma**, which means "form, appearance, or shape." This activity can help students understand how the structure and formation of words (morphology) and their meanings (semantics) are related. Visualizing these relationships in a chart makes learning more explicit and illustrates the interconnectedness of language subsystems.

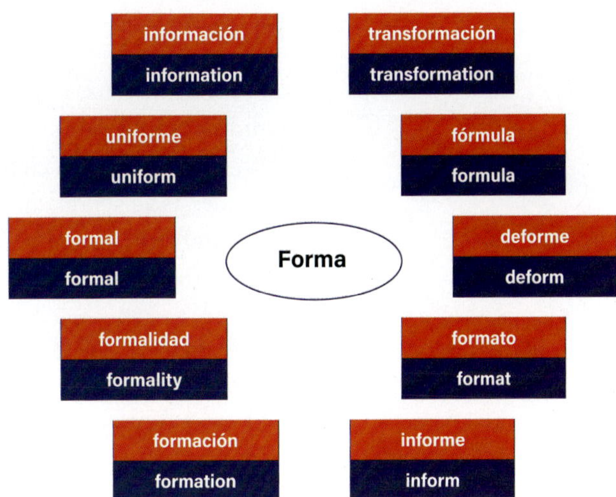

Content Knowledge Cognate Interactive Display

Leveraging technology to match English and Spanish cognates is also beneficial. Using this interactive display, students identify the word's equivalent in the other language, simultaneously building content-area vocabulary and knowledge in both languages.

Cognates	Cognados
words that have the same meaning and are pronounced and spelled almost the same in two different languages	**palabras que se pronuncian y se escriben casi igual y significan lo mismo en dos idiomas**
carbon	cultivar
glucose	generar
cultivate	emisiones
generate	carbono
consumption	etanol
emissions	glucosa
ethanol	fotosíntesis
photosynthesis	consumo

In Action

Mr. Ruiz and Mrs. López share a dual-language Grade 2 and Grade 3 combination class. They are teaching a literature unit with an emphasis on characterization. The teachers want students to understand synonyms and antonyms, knowing that it will increase their oral and written vocabularies and enhance their ability to discern the meaning of words in context.

Spanish to English Lesson: Antonyms

To begin, students will learn about antonyms in Spanish and then they will use a routine to explore the equivalency of terms across languages.

<table>
<tr><th colspan="3">Paso 1: Usar lo que ya sabemos y hemos aprendido sobre el español</th></tr>
<tr><td>Establecer el objetivo de la lección y la relación de transferencia</td><td>Hoy vamos a comparar y contrastar los antónimos en español y en inglés. Vamos a repasar cómo funcionan y cómo se usan los antónimos tanto en español como en inglés.</td><td rowspan="2">Los antónimos son palabras opuestas. Quieren decir lo contrario.<table><tr><td>bueno</td><td></td></tr><tr><td>lindo</td><td></td></tr><tr><td>valiente</td><td></td></tr><tr><td>feliz</td><td></td></tr><tr><td>trabajador</td><td></td></tr><tr><td>agradable</td><td></td></tr><tr><td>generoso</td><td></td></tr><tr><td>inteligente</td><td></td></tr><tr><td>justo</td><td></td></tr><tr><td>maravilloso</td><td></td></tr></table></td></tr>
<tr><td>Repasar la definición y función de los antónimos</td><td>Recuerden que los antónimos son un par de palabras con significado opuesto. Una palabra opuesta quiere decir lo contrario de otra.
Muestre un bolsillero con adjetivos escritos en tarjetas.

Todas estas palabras se pueden usar para describir a los personajes en los cuentos. Esta primera columna tiene cualidades positivas o admirables.</td></tr>
<tr><td>Confirmar el concepto: lo repasado y aprendido</td><td>Lea cada palabra y pida a los estudiantes que la lean a coro.

Repita con todas las palabras.
La palabra es ________
¿Qué palabra?
Luego coloque la palabra opuesta al lado según dice:
Lo opuesto de _____ es _____.
Repita con todas las palabras.

Los antónimos son pares de palabras opuestas. Una palabra opuesta significa lo contrario de la otra palabra.</td><td>Los antónimos son palabras opuestas. Quieren decir lo contrario.<table><tr><td>bueno</td><td>malo</td></tr><tr><td>lindo</td><td>feo</td></tr><tr><td>valiente</td><td>cobarde</td></tr><tr><td>feliz</td><td>triste</td></tr><tr><td>trabajador</td><td>perezoso</td></tr><tr><td>agradable</td><td>desagradable</td></tr><tr><td>generoso</td><td>egoísta</td></tr><tr><td>inteligente</td><td>tonto</td></tr><tr><td>justo</td><td>injusto</td></tr><tr><td>maravilloso</td><td>terrible</td></tr></table></td></tr>
</table>

Paso 2: Conectar, comparar y contrastar con el inglés

Preparación de manipulativos Promover conocimientos previos y asociaciones	Use el bolsillero con las palabras en español para demostrar sus equivalentes en inglés. *¿Creen que en inglés también existen las palabras opuestas?*
Colaboración y trabajo en pares o grupos	Vaya colocando la palabra en inglés al lado de la palabra en español. Pregunte: *¿Cómo se dice _______ en inglés?* (Los estudiantes contestan en inglés). Entre compañeros En pares o grupos pequeños invite a los estudiantes a correlacionar las palabras para crear pares de antónimos en inglés y en español. Motive a los estudiantes a escoger las palabras del bolsillero para crear un tablero de antónimos en español y en inglés.
Invitar a los estudiantes a compartir conocimientos	Juegos Pida a los estudiantes que inventen juegos con tarjetas de antónimos en inglés y en español. Por ejemplo, se reparten tarjetas de antónimos en español. Cada estudiante toma un turno para escoger una tarjeta. Para ganar 4 puntos, dicho estudiante tiene que decir las palabras opuestas en inglés y en español que se generan de esa palabra: valiente: brave – cobarde: coward.
Afirmar la comparación y contraste entre ambos idiomas	*Compartan con un compañero lo que han aprendido sobre los antónimos en español y en inglés.*

Palabras equivalentes en inglés

bueno	good
lindo	beautiful
valiente	brave
feliz	happy
maravilloso	wonderful
amigable	friendly
generoso	generous
amable	kind
inteligente	intelligent
malo	bad
feo	ugly
cobarde	coward
triste	sad
perezoso	lazy
egoísta	selfish
tonto	silly
injusto	unfair
terrible	terrible

Entre compañeros

Antónimos en español		Antónimos en inglés	
bueno	malo	good	bad

Juegos

cobarde

valiente

brave

coward

Paso 3: Promover destrezas metalingüísticas al resumir lo aprendido				
Resumir lo aprendido	Muestre el organizador gráfico para resumir lo aprendido sobre los antónimos en español y en inglés. Pida a pares de estudiantes que expliquen lo que aprendieron. Pregunte: *¿Qué hemos aprendido sobre los antónimos en español y en inglés?*	Español	Ambos	Inglés
		Cada palabra que forma el par de antónimos es específica al español.	Existe la relación entre palabras antónimas. Los antónimos son pares de palabras opuestas. Significan lo contrario una de la otra palabra.	Cada palabra que forma el par de antónimos es específica al inglés.
Afirmar la lectoescritura bilingüe y las conexiones con el inglés	*Ya aprendieron que los antónimos son pares de palabras opuestas. Esto quiere decir que cada palabra significa lo contrario de la otra. Tanto en inglés como en español, los antónimos se usan mucho para describir; son adjetivos que describen a las personas, animales, ideas o cosas. Sin embargo, los términos o palabras que expresan los significados opuestos son específicos a cada idioma.*			

Semantics is integral to language development.

English to Spanish Lesson: Antonyms and Synonyms

Mr. Ruiz and Mrs. López will continue exploring synonyms and antonyms with their students in the coming units. Now Mr. Ruiz will build on the Spanish to English bridging lesson by comparing and contrasting synonyms in English and Spanish, noting that synonyms and antonyms are word relationships that exist in both English and Spanish, yet the terms used are specific to each language.

<table>
<tr><th colspan="4">Step 1: Review what we know and have learned about English</th></tr>
<tr><td rowspan="9">State Lesson Objective

Review Concepts Already Learned About English</td><td rowspan="9">Today we are going to review antonyms and synonyms, which we know are word relationships that exist in both English and Spanish.

Display a chart to contextualize and review the meaning of the academic terms.

In both English and Spanish there are antonyms and synonyms. Antonyms are word pairs that have opposite meanings. Synonyms are word pairs that have the same meaning.

We have already learned antonym pairs in English and Spanish. Next we are going to explore synonyms. These are pairs of words that have the same meaning.</td><td colspan="2">Antonym</td></tr>
<tr><td>anti or anto means "against"</td><td>nym means "name or word"</td></tr>
<tr><td colspan="2">Antonyms are words that have opposite meanings.</td></tr>
<tr><td>big</td><td>small</td></tr>
<tr><td colspan="2">Synonym</td></tr>
<tr><td>syn means "the same"</td><td>nym means "name or word"</td></tr>
<tr><td colspan="2">Synonyms are words that have the same meaning.</td></tr>
<tr><td>big</td><td>large</td></tr>
<tr><td colspan="2"></td></tr>
<tr><td rowspan="12">Model by Brainstorming and Listing Synonyms

Affirm the Reviewed and Learned Concepts</td><td rowspan="12">Display a list of words and elicit students' responses for each word on the list.

What is another word that means the same as or has a very similar meaning to _____?

Remind students that there may be more than one word that is similar in meaning to another. So some words may have more than one synonym.

Turn to your partner and tell them what you know and have learned about synonyms.

Provide a response frame if necessary:

Synonyms are words that mean the _____ or have _____ meanings. One word can have more than one _____.</td><td colspan="2">Synonym</td></tr>
<tr><td colspan="2">words that mean the same or have very similar meanings</td></tr>
<tr><td>small</td><td>little, tiny</td></tr>
<tr><td>happy</td><td>content, jolly</td></tr>
<tr><td>sad</td><td>unhappy, gloomy</td></tr>
<tr><td>good</td><td>fine</td></tr>
<tr><td>angry</td><td>cross, mad</td></tr>
<tr><td>old</td><td>elderly, ancient</td></tr>
<tr><td>wrong</td><td>incorrect</td></tr>
<tr><td>fast</td><td>speedy, quick</td></tr>
<tr><td>answer</td><td>response, reply</td></tr>
<tr><td>beautiful</td><td>pretty, attractive, gorgeous</td></tr>
</table>

Step 2: Connect, compare, and contrast to Spanish

Model	Next, compare and contrast synonyms in English and Spanish. *Do you think synonyms also exist in Spanish? Do some words in Spanish have the same or similar meanings?*
Promote Prior Knowledge and Use of All Linguistic Resources Collaboration	Display a list of the synonyms reviewed in English. Ask students to brainstorm the equivalent synonyms in Spanish. Record and post brainstormed answers. *In both English and Spanish, synonyms are very useful in choosing exactly the best word for what you want to express.* Invite students to work in pairs using the brainstormed list as reference. First, have them replace the underlined words with synonyms in English. Then, translate the sentence into Spanish. **The old man walked fast with a small dog.** (El anciano caminaba rápido con un perrito pequeño). **He was happy because he had the right answers.** (El estaba contento porque tenía las respuestas correctas).
Compare and Contrast English and Spanish	Motivate student pairs to create their own sentences to present to the whole group. Have students explore using different synonyms and choosing the ones they like best. Remind students that most synonyms are adjectives. *In Spanish, the adjectives must agree in gender and number with the noun they describe.* *Also, in Spanish the adjective is placed after the noun it describes.*

English	Spanish
small little tiny	pequeño chiquito minúsculo
happy content jolly	feliz contento alegre
sad unhappy gloomy	triste entristecido melancólico
good fine	bueno bien
angry cross mad	enfadado irritado enojado
old elderly ancient	viejo mayor de edad anciano
fast speedy quick	rápido veloz ágil
answer reply	contestación respuesta
beautiful pretty attractive	hermoso lindo atractivo

The old man walked fast with a small dog.

El anciano caminaba rápido con un perrito pequeño.

El viejo caminaba veloz con un perrito chiquito.

Step 3: Promote metalinguistic skills by summarizing what was learned				
Summarize What Was Learned	Show an anchor chart to summarize what was learned about synonyms in English and in Spanish. *What did we learn about synonyms in English? What did we learn about synonyms in Spanish?* *What are important differences to notice between synonyms in English and Spanish?* *Why are synonyms important to writers and translators?* *What reference materials or applications can we use to find synonyms quickly?*	**English** Synonyms in English are neutral and do not have to agree in gender and number with the noun they modify. When a synonym is an adjective, it is placed before the noun it modifies.	**Both** Synonyms are words that have the same or similar meanings. Most synonyms are adjectives used to describe nouns or adverbs used to describe verbs.	**Spanish** In Spanish, when a synonym is an adjective, it must agree in gender and number with the noun it modifies. When a synonym is an adjective, it is placed after the noun it describes.
Affirm Biliteracy and Cross-Linguistic Connections	*Now you know that you can use synonyms in English and in Spanish to choose a word that expresses best what you want to convey.* *In English and Spanish, writers use a print or online dictionary to look up synonyms when they write—to help them choose a word that means exactly what they want to say. Translators also use dictionaries to look up the synonyms of words to make sure their translations convey the same meaning in both languages.*			

Synonyms help writers convey meaning accurately.

Assessment Considerations

Assessing whether students know the same vocabulary in two different languages involves evaluating their language proficiency and understanding of corresponding terms. To avoid redundancy and over-assessing, teachers should judiciously assign assessment tasks that are asset-oriented and that encourage students to use all their linguistic resources as well as reference tools such as dictionaries, thesauruses, and classroom texts. In this way, teachers promote student agency and provide opportunities for students to monitor their own learning.

Promote student agency with peer and self-assessments.

Here are several ways to assess vocabulary across languages.

Assessment Tool	Description
Vocabulary Matching	Create a list of vocabulary words in both languages and ask students to match the equivalent terms. This can be done using student-created vocabulary cards or an interactive whiteboard.
Picture or Image Identification (Oral or Written)	Use images or pictures to represent vocabulary items and ask students to identify and label them in both languages. This method is especially effective for concrete nouns.
Contextual Usage	Present sentences or paragraphs with specific vocabulary terms underlined. Students replace the underlined word in the other language.
Definitions	Provide a set of definitions and have students give the corresponding term in both languages.
Crossword Puzzles	Create puzzles with clues or words in one language and the corresponding answers or translations in the other. This adds an element of fun to the assessment.
Peer or Self-Assessment	Encourage students to assess their own oral or written vocabulary knowledge or to swap assessments with classmates to check each other's understanding.

Caveat

When designing assessments, remember to consider students' proficiency levels, the complexity of the vocabulary, and the context in which the languages are used.

Provide differentiated assessment by giving options that reflect the language development continuum with substantial, moderate, or minimal support as needed.

Pause and Reflect

How can studying semantics help with making inferences?

What kinds of vocabulary charts or logs are you going to use?

Conclusion

In conclusion, semantics plays a crucial role in cross-linguistic teaching and learning. The study of semantics extends beyond individual words, encompassing word relationships, contextual understanding, word families, word usage, precision, and conceptual understanding. It is important to teach vocabulary and word knowledge through explicit instruction. While some conceptual knowledge can transfer easily from one language to another, explicit instruction is still needed to build content-area vocabulary and to understand nuanced language.

The concept of equivalency is also vital for effective communication and translation between languages. This extends beyond vocabulary and concepts, as the challenges posed by cultural and linguistic differences are complex.

Strong semantic skills are critical stepping stones to achieving biliteracy. Proficient semantic skills facilitate comprehension, inferencing, and overall literacy development. When students gain an appreciation for and an understanding of the cultural nuances of language, they can communicate, read, and write more effectively. To accomplish this, it is necessary to study word relationships and equivalencies with intentionality.

 |

Key Takeaways

Semantics and cross-linguistic vocabulary instruction extend beyond individual words, encompassing word relationships, contextual understanding, word families, word usage, precision, and conceptual understanding.

Equivalency refers to the idea that different languages have words or terms that represent the same or similar concepts.

Word relationships are equivalent constructs or concepts in English and Spanish. While word-relation categories may be the same in both languages, the specific terms or words that represent these relationships are different and specific to each language.

Vocabulary and word relationships need to be taught explicitly.

Assessing students' vocabulary development in two different languages involves evaluating their language proficiency and their understanding of corresponding terms.

Chapter 9

Grammar and Syntax

"If you talk to a man in a language he understands, that goes to his head.

"If you talk to him in his language, that goes to his heart."

"Si le hablas a un hombre en un idioma que entiende, eso le llegará a su mente.

Si le hablas en su idioma, eso le llegará al corazón".

–Nelson Mandela, 2011

Chapter 9 focuses on the importance of grammar and syntax as subsystems and their roles in effective oral and written communication. Grammar and syntax are two closely related concepts that are essential to biliteracy.

Comparisons of general versus specific features of English and Spanish grammar and syntax are described in his chapter. Both parallel language frames and analysis are explored as effective strategies to facilitate language development and cross-linguistic connections. Finally, the chapter will discuss how writing tasks with prompts can be used to assess cross-linguistic transfer in these subsystems.

In This Chapter

> The purpose of grammar is to facilitate effective communication by providing a standardized framework that allows speakers and writers to convey their ideas clearly and accurately.

Grammar and Syntax

Grammar refers to the set of rules and conventions that govern the structure and use of language. It encompasses the principles and guidelines for constructing sentences, organizing words, and conveying meaning in a coherent and systematic way. Grammar includes syntax (sentence structure) and interrelates with other language subsystems such as morphology (word formation and inflections), phonology (sound patterns), and semantics (meaning of words and sentences), but it is mostly related to the function of words in a sentence.

The purpose of grammar is to facilitate effective communication by providing a standardized framework that allows speakers and writers to convey their ideas clearly and accurately. Different languages have their own specific grammatical rules, and adherence to these rules helps ensure that messages are conveyed in a way that is understandable and meaningful to others. While some aspects of grammar are universal, there can be significant variations between languages in terms of their grammatical structures and rules.

In linguistics, syntax is a branch of grammar that encompasses the set of rules for the combination of punctuation, words, and phrases to form well-structured sentences or expressions in a language. Syntax involves analyzing these components to understand how meaning is conveyed. It is a fundamental aspect of grammar and language structure.

Grammar, Syntax, and Biliteracy

Grammar plays a crucial role in developing biliteracy. Understanding grammar helps learners make sense of language structures and elements such as sentence formation, word order, and the use of tenses in each language. This is fundamental for creating coherent and grammatically correct sentences in both languages.

Grammatical awareness is related to oral and written expression. In both Spanish and English, syntax involves the arrangement of words and phrases to form grammatically correct sentences. Understanding the structure of language and how to construct and express ideas cohesively in each language is critical for achieving biliteracy. When students understand the rules that govern word order and sentence structure, and agreement, they can craft comprehensible language.

Understanding grammar helps learners make sense of language structures.

Learn More

Ballinger, S., Man Chu Lau, S., & Quevillon Lacasse, C. (2020). Cross-linguistic pedagogy: Harnessing transfer in the classroom. *Canadian Modern Language Review, 76*(4), 265–277.

National Clearinghouse for English Language Acquisition. Family Toolkit. https://ncela.ed.gov/educator-support/toolkits/family-toolkit

Caveat

While some aspects of grammar are universal, there can be significant variations between languages in terms of their grammatical structures and rules.

It cannot be assumed that language learners will unravel complex language structures without explicit teaching of cross-linguistic transfer elements focusing on the forms and function of each language.

When students understand a grammatical construct or skill in their native language, it will be easier for them to understand it in their new language. If grammar skills are not understood in the native language, they will not easily transfer to the new language.

In a bilingual classroom, students often need to navigate academic materials in both languages. A solid foundation in grammar supports academic success by facilitating effective communication and comprehension across various subjects. This is essential in creating and expressing coherent and grammatically correct sentences in both languages.

Biliteracy requires cognitive flexibility to switch seamlessly between two languages. Syntax helps in this regard by serving as a framework that aids in this switching process. Knowledge of syntax in one language can be transferred to another. When students are literate in one language, they can use their understanding of syntactic structures as a foundation for learning and mastering the syntax of a second language. This transferable knowledge accelerates the development of grammatical and syntactical awareness skills leading to biliteracy.

Key Terms

Grammar: The set of rules and conventions that govern the structure and use of language.

Syntax: A branch of grammar that encompasses the set of rules for the combination of punctuation, words, and phrases to form well-structured sentences or expressions in a language.

Parts of Speech: The basic categories of words based on their grammatical forms and syntactic functions within a sentence.

Cross-Linguistic Connections

Recall that English and Spanish are both Indo-European languages, but they belong to different branches of the language family: English is Germanic, while Spanish is Romance, meaning from the Roman language Latin. As a result, they exhibit some similarities but also significant differences in their grammatical forms. This makes cross-linguistic connections complex because some aspects are transferable while others are not.

Parts of speech are the basic categories of words based on their grammatical forms and syntactic functions within a sentence. This chart (not all inclusive) compares and contrasts some elements of the parts of speech in Spanish and English.

Definition and Commonalities	English	Spanish
Noun A noun is a word that represents a person, place, thing, or idea. Nouns can be singular or plural.	There is no grammatical gender for nouns (*teacher, school, book, knowledge*). Rules for pluralization of nouns are more varied in English.	Nouns have grammatical gender and are classified as masculine or feminine (maestro/a, escuela, libro, conocimiento). Rules for pluralization include adding -s or -es and changing the ending from z to c and adding -es.
Pronoun A pronoun is a word that is used to replace a noun. Personal pronouns represent different persons (first, second, and third) and numbers (singular and plural). Both languages distinguish between subject pronouns (used as the subject of a sentence) and object pronouns (used as the object of a verb or preposition).	Seven subject pronouns are used (I, you, he, she, it, we, they).	Nine subject pronouns are used (Yo, tú, él, ella, nosotros, vosotros, ellos, ellas, ustedes). Spanish has both formal and informal forms of the second-person singular pronoun "you." Tú" is used informally, while "usted" is used formally, especially in situations of respect or with strangers. Subject pronouns are often omitted.
Article An article is a word that is placed before a noun to show if it is specific or general.	Articles do not change based on the gender or number of the noun (definite "the" and indefinite "a" or "an").	Articles (definite "el," "la," "los," "las" and indefinite "un," "una," "unos," "unas") must agree with the gender and number of the noun(s) they modify.

Table continues on next page

Definition and Commonalities	English	Spanish
Verb This is a word that expresses an action or a state of being. Both languages conjugate verbs based on the subject of the sentence. Both languages express various tenses, such as past, present, future.	Specific tenses and the ways they are formed can vary. Auxiliary verbs are frequently used. Subject pronouns are generally required for clarity.	Specific tenses and the ways they are formed can vary. Auxiliary verbs are seldom used. Subject pronouns are frequently omitted because the verb conjugation already indicates the subject.
Adjective This is a word that describes or modifies a noun or pronoun.	Adjectives precede the noun they modify. There is a specific order for placement of adjectives in a sentence.	Adjectives usually come after the noun they describe.
Adverb This is a word that modifies a verb, adjective, or another adverb. Adverbs can be formed from adjectives, in most cases by adding a specific suffix.	Adverbs are usually placed after the verb. There are some equivalent adverbs (soon—pronto), but depending on context, they may not always convey the same meaning.	Adverbs can be placed after the verb, but also at the beginning or end of the sentence for emphasis. There are some equivalent adverbs (cerca—near), but depending on context, they may not always convey the same meaning.
Conjunction This is a word that connects words, phrases, or clauses in a sentence.	Conjunctions typically come between the words, phrases, or clauses they connect. They do not always have direct equivalents in Spanish.	A conjunction can come before or after the words, phrases, or clauses it connects. Conjunctions do not always have direct equivalents in English.
Preposition This is a word that shows the relationship between a noun or pronoun and other elements in a sentence. Prepositions indicate relationships between elements in a sentence, such as time, location, direction, possession. Prepositions typically precede their objects.	Prepositions do not always have direct equivalents in Spanish. Different prepositions are used to convey ideas across languages.	Prepositions do not have direct equivalents in English. Different prepositions are used to convey ideas across languages. Spanish prepositions often require the use of object pronouns (me, te, le, nos, os, les), as in: Te estoy esperando arriba. I am waiting for you up here.
Interjection This is a word or phrase that expresses strong and spontaneous emotion or surprise.	Interjections are culturally specific, reflecting the nuances of the speakers over time. Punctuation of interjections is specific to each language.	Interjections are culturally specific, reflecting the nuances of the speakers over time. Punctuation is specific to each language.

Types of Sentences

In both English and Spanish, sentences can be classified into various types based on their structure and purpose.

Common Purpose	English	Spanish
To make a statement or express an opinion	Declarative sentence	Oración declarativa
To ask a question	Interrogative sentence	Oración interrogativa
To give commands or instructions	Imperative sentence	Oración imperativa
To express strong emotion	Exclamatory sentence	Oración exclamativa

In both English and Spanish, declarative sentences start with a capital letter and finish with a period. However, when asking a question, Spanish uses two question marks: one upside down (¿) at the beginning of the sentence and one at the end (?). In English, only one question mark is used, and it is placed at the end.

For sentences that give commands (imperatives) or express strong emotions (exclamations), Spanish uses both an opening (¡) and closing (!) exclamation point, while English places the exclamation point only at the end of such sentences.

English	Type of Sentence	Spanish
You finished the project on time.	Declarative	Terminaste el proyecto a tiempo.
Did you finish the project on time?	Interrogative	¿Terminaste el proyecto a tiempo?
Finish the project on time!	Imperative	¡Termina el proyecto a tiempo!
You finished the project on time!	Exclamatory	¡Terminaste el proyecto a tiempo!

Formation and Structure of Sentences

Understanding the different types of sentences helps in effective communication and writing, as each type serves a specific purpose in conveying information or expressing ideas. In both English and Spanish, simple, compound, complex, and compound-complex sentences serve similar functions. However, while the basic structures of these sentence types are similar in English and Spanish, there may be differences in word order, punctuation, and the use of specific conjunctions.

Definition	English	Spanish
Simple Sentence consists of one independent clause, expressing a complete thought	The hare ran fast.	La liebre corrió rápido.
Compound Sentence consists of two or more independent clauses joined by a coordinating conjunction (for, and, but, or, yet, so)	The hare runs fast, but he lost the race.	La liebre corrió rápido, pero perdió la carrera.
Complex Sentence contains an independent clause and one or more dependent clauses, joined by a subordinating conjunction (because, since, until)	Although the tortoise was slow, she continued one step after the next, and eventually she won the race.	Aunque la tortuga era lenta, siguió paso a paso, y eventualmente ganó la carrera.
Compound-Complex Sentence contains two independent clauses joined by a comma-conjunction and contains at least one dependent clause	The hare took a nap, only to wake up and see that the tortoise had already won the race.	La liebre se acostó a dormir, y se despertó para encontrar que la tortuga ya había ganado la carrera.

Parallel Language Frames

Language frames, commonly known as sentence frames or response prompts, play a significant role in language acquisition. The frame provides a structured or partially completed sentence that serves as a model for constructing new sentences.

Teachers use parallel sentence or response frames to emphasize their use and form across languages. During cross-linguistic transfer instruction, the parallel language frames are displayed and analyzed. When teachers show frames side-by-side, students gain proficient use of the structures that apply in each language.

The use of parallel sentence frames contributes to the development of biliteracy in several ways, including:

Comparative Sentence Type and Structure

Parallel sentence and response frames offer a clear structure for learners to follow, helping them understand the grammatical rules and sentence construction patterns of each language.

Example: Understanding Adjective Placement

English	Spanish
I see a beautiful, tall, green tree from here.	Desde aquí veo un árbol hermoso, alto y verde.

Contextual Learning and Application

Sentence frames provide context for language use. Learners can see how words and phrases are used in real-life situations, enhancing their ability to comprehend and apply language in different contexts.

Example: Language Function

English	Spanish
I agree with you, but would like to add _____.	Estoy de acuerdo contigo, pero quisiera añadir que _____.

Oral and Written Communication

Using sentence frames helps learners develop their communication skills by providing a structure for expressing thoughts and ideas. This can be particularly helpful for those who are still building their confidence in writing and speaking a new language.

Example: Stating Opinions

English	Spanish
In my opinion, _____.	En mi opinión _____.

Cultural Relevance

Sentence frames can incorporate culturally relevant content, allowing learners not only to grasp the language but also understand the cultural nuances associated with specific expressions and communication styles.

Example: Courtesy Language

English	Spanish
I am pleased to meet you.	Estoy encantado de conocerle.

Sentence and response frames serve as valuable tools in language acquisition by offering structured support, fostering contextual understanding, and facilitating the gradual development of linguistic skills. When analyzed side-by-side during cross-linguistic instructional time, parallel language frames provide an opportunity for students to better understand the similarities and differences in academic language structures that facilitate academic oral and written expression in each language.

Common Parallel Language Frames

English	Spanish
To share a new idea or opinion	**Para compartir una idea u opinión**
I think that _____.	Creo que _____.
I notice that _____.	Noto que _____.
My opinion is _____.	Mi opinión es que _____.
Something important to know is _____.	Algo importante que debemos saber es que _____.
To gain the floor	**Para tomar la palabra**
I would like to add _____.	Me gustaría añadir que _____.
Excuse me for interrupting, but _____.	Disculpen por interrumpir, pero _____.
That made me think of _____.	Eso me hace pensar que _____.
To build on a peer's idea or opinion	**Para ampliar la idea u opinión de un compañero**
I also think that _____.	También creo que _____.
In addition, _____.	Además, _____.
Another idea is _____.	Otra idea es que _____.
To express agreement with a peer's idea	**Para expresar acuerdo con la idea de un compañero**
I agree with _____ because _____.	Estoy de acuerdo con _____ porque _____.
I agree that _____.	Estoy de acuerdo en que _____.
I think that is important because _____.	Pienso que eso es importante porque _____.
To express respectful disagreement	**Para expresar desacuerdo con respeto**
I disagree with _____ because _____.	No estoy de acuerdo con _____ porque _____.
I understand your point, but I think _____.	Entiendo tu punto de vista, pero creo que _____.
Have you considered that _____?	¿Has considerado que _____?
To ask a clarifying question	**Para hacer una pregunta aclaratoria**
What did you mean when you said _____?	¿Qué quisiste decir cuando dijiste _____?
Are you saying that _____ or that _____?	¿Estás diciendo que _____ o que _____?
Can you explain what you mean by _____?	¿Puedes explicar lo que quieres decir con _____?
To clarify for others	**Para aclarar lo que quieres expresar a los demás**
I mean that _____.	Quise decir que _____.
I am trying to say that _____.	Estoy tratando de decir que _____.
Let me give you an example: _____.	Déjenme darles un ejemplo: _____.

Using Parallel Texts

Using parallel text translations for linguistic analysis or close reading offers several advantages, particularly in the context of cross-linguistic transfer. Parallel texts allow for a direct comparison of linguistic structures between two languages. This is particularly useful for syntactic and morphological analysis. Teachers can identify similarities and differences in sentence structures, word order, and grammatical constructions to help students analyze text and understand how each language encodes meaning.

Parallel texts can be valuable resources for language learners. Learners can use parallel texts to improve their understanding of grammar, vocabulary, and idiomatic expressions by noticing how they are used in context across languages.

In addition, parallel texts provide insight into cultural differences and similarities by revealing how concepts and ideas are expressed differently across languages. This facilitates cross-cultural analysis, enabling students to explore cultural norms, values, and perspectives embedded in language use. Side-by-side analysis of the translations allows students to evaluate their own choices, learn from alternative translations, and develop strategies for handling difficult linguistic and cultural challenges.

However, keep in mind that the use of parallel texts is limited to the study of contrastive analysis. Teachers use sections of the texts to compare and contrast linguistic features across languages during a designated cross-linguistic transfer time.

The benefits and impact of parallel text have been documented since the early 2000s (Bolaños Cuéllar, 2007; Conti, 2015; Cummins, 2021). These benefits extend beyond syntactical analysis and include some of the following:

- They encourage cross-linguistic noticing.
- They effectively scaffold reading for less proficient or less confident readers.
- They promote academic vocabulary in parallel and authentic contexts.
- They facilitate access to complex text and support differentiation.
- They provide a way to connect, compare, and contrast text across languages.

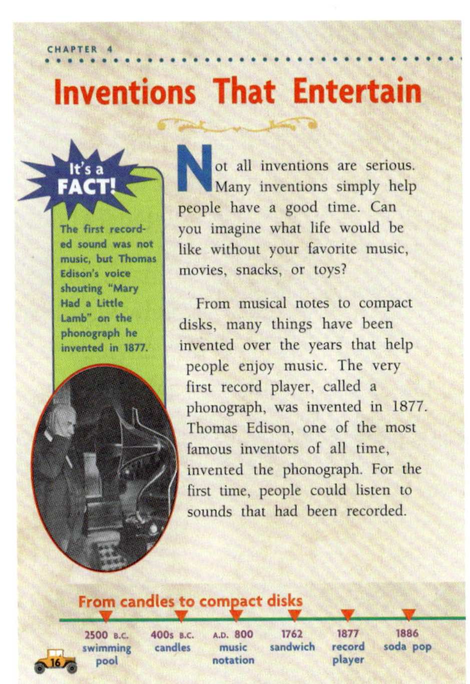

CHAPTER 4

Inventions That Entertain

It's a FACT!

The first recorded sound was not music, but Thomas Edison's voice shouting "Mary Had a Little Lamb" on the phonograph he invented in 1877.

Not all inventions are serious. Many inventions simply help people have a good time. Can you imagine what life would be like without your favorite music, movies, snacks, or toys?

From musical notes to compact disks, many things have been invented over the years that help people enjoy music. The very first record player, called a phonograph, was invented in 1877. Thomas Edison, one of the most famous inventors of all time, invented the phonograph. For the first time, people could listen to sounds that had been recorded.

From candles to compact disks

2500 B.C. swimming pool · 400s B.C. candles · A.D. 800 music notation · 1762 sandwich · 1877 record player · 1886 soda pop

16

CAPÍTULO 4

Inventos para divertirse

¡Así fue!

Los primeros sonidos que se grabaron no fueron de música, sino la voz de Thomas Edison cantando a gritos "María tenía un corderito", en el fonógrafo que inventó en 1877.

No todos los inventos son tan serios. Muchos simplemente permiten que la gente se divierta. ¿Te imaginas cómo sería la vida sin tu música, tus películas o tus juguetes favoritos?

Desde las notas musicales hasta los discos compactos, muchas cosas se han inventado a lo largo de los años que ayudan a disfrutar de la música. El primer tocadiscos, al que se llamó "fonógrafo", fue inventado en 1877. Lo inventó Thomas Edison, uno de los inventores más famosos de todos los tiempos. Gracias a su invento, la gente podía escuchar por primera vez sonidos grabados previamente.

De la vela a los discos compactos

2500 AC la piscina · 400 AC la vela · 800 DC la notación musical · 1762 el sándwich · 1877 el tocadiscos · 1886 los refrescos

16

Examples of English-Spanish parallel texts
© Benchmark Education Company LLC

In Action

Mrs. Cowen, the English Language Arts teacher and Mrs. Vásquez, the Spanish Language Arts teacher realize the advantage of using parallel text analysis during their cross-linguistic instructional time in their combination Grade 4 and Grade 5 classroom. Together, they choose a parallel passage aligned to the topic theme of their unit on technology. Then they analyze the passage using each of the language subsystems to determine which standards-based skills they will emphasize and in which language.

They used this **language subsystem planning tool** to follow a process for connecting, comparing, and contrasting one text to the other:

1. **Phonology/Orthography:** Identify interesting sound-spelling relationships and letter patterns appropriate to their grade level, and their impact on syllabic stress patterns.
2. **Morphology:** Choose words to explore for comparative word analysis, root words, prefixes, suffixes, cognates, and their derivatives.
3. **Semantics:** Conduct a word-level analysis by selecting content-specific vocabulary, general academic vocabulary, cognates, transition words, and/or multiple-meaning words that need to be emphasized.
4. **Syntax:** Recognize sentence structures to analyze and deconstruct.
5. **Grammar:** Notice specific grammar features and forms that appear in the text.
6. **Pragmatics:** Identify notable phrases, idioms, and embedded cultural nuances.
7. **Whole Text:** Identify the general text features—headings, subheadings, captions, illustrations, diagrams, timetables—and language-specific conventions each text offers.

Next, they decide which of the identified language elements will be taught for transfer in each language. Both teachers feel that working at the sentence level will benefit students the most.

Spanish to English Lesson: Complex Sentences

Mrs. Vásquez wants to use the text as a model for teaching complex sentences. Mrs. Cowen will use the appositive phrase (a noun phrase that follows another noun phrase and provides additional information about the noun) found in the text for the cross-linguistic transfer from English to Spanish.

Paso 1: Usar lo que ya sabemos y hemos aprendido sobre el español		
Establecer el objetivo de la lección y la relación de transferencia Repasar la definición de las oraciones complejas Confirmar el concepto, lo repasado y lo aprendido	*Hoy vamos a analizar las oraciones complejas para determinar si tienen la misma estructura en español y en inglés.* Explique mientras anota: *Una oración compleja tiene tres partes: una cláusula adverbial que comienza con un adverbio (desde).* *Una oración o cláusula independiente que contiene un sujeto (cosas) y un verbo (se han inventado), más una cláusula dependiente que comienza con una conjunción (que).* Compare el texto en español con el de inglés: Identifique las tres partes, el adverbio (from) en la primera cláusula, el sujeto (things) y el verbo (have been invented) en la oración o cláusula dependiente. La conjunción (that) para comenzar la última cláusula, dependiente. *¿Qué observamos?*	Una oración compleja tiene tres partes: 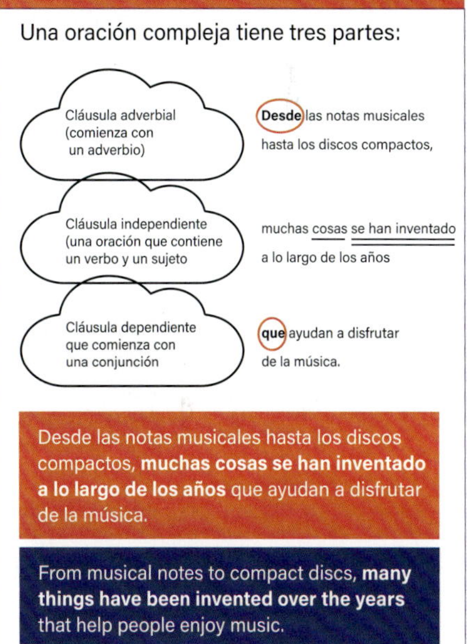

Paso 2: Conectar, comparar y contrastar con el inglés

Colaboración y trabajo en pares o grupos	*Ahora ustedes van a escribir una oración compleja en español y en inglés. Luego, las leeremos y las compartiremos.*
Promover conocimientos previos y asociaciones	Observe a los estudiantes mientras trabajan y oriéntelos cuando sea necesario. *Pueden traducir sus oraciones o escribir una oración distinta en cada idioma.* Muestre una lista de adverbios en español y en inglés.
Invitar a los estudiantes a compartir conocimientos con un compañero	Invite a los estudiantes a compartir sus oraciones. *¿Cuáles son las tres partes de una oración compleja tanto en español como en inglés?*
Afirmar la comparación y contraste entre ambos idiomas	Respuesta: *Tanto en inglés como en español, una oración compleja tiene tres partes: una cláusula adverbial que comienza con un adverbio. Una oración o cláusula independiente que contiene un sujeto y un verbo. Y una cláusula dependiente que comienza con una conjunción.*

Antes de ir al parque, tengo que terminar mi tarea **porque** quiero sacar buenas notas.

Before I go to the park, I must finish my homework **because** I want to get good grades.

Ejemplo de posibles respuestas:

Maybe I will not be able to go to your house, I must take care of my little sister, **but** tomorrow I will be able to come over.

Quizás no pueda ir a tu casa, tengo que cuidar a mi hermanita, **pero** mañana si voy a poder ir.

Adverbios	Adverbs
aquí	here
allá	there
antes	before
después	after
luego	later
quizás	maybe
nunca	never

Paso 3: Promover destrezas metalingüísticas al resumir lo aprendido

Resumir lo aprendido	*¿Qué hemos aprendido hoy? Hemos aprendido que tanto en inglés como en español las oraciones complejas tienen la misma estructura. Las oraciones complejas tienen tres partes: Una frase o clausula adverbial, una oración completa y una cláusula o frase independiente.*
Afirmar la lectoescritura bilingüe y las conexiones con el inglés	*Las oraciones complejas se llaman complejas porque expresan varios pensamientos a la vez. El poder expresarse oralmente o por escrito con oraciones complejas bien estructuradas es un gran logro académico. ¡Poder hacerlo en dos idiomas es un logro doble!*

English to Spanish Lesson: Appositives

In the parallel text, Mrs. Cowen noticed an appositive and wanted to plan a brief cross-linguistic transfer lesson on the structure of appositives in English and Spanish.

Step 1: Review what we know and have learned about English		
State Lesson Objective Review Concepts Already Learned About English Affirm the Reviewed and Learned Concepts	*Today we are going to review the structure of appositives. We will explore appositives in English and in Spanish.* Display a chart to review appositives: *An appositive is a noun phrase that comes before another noun phrase to describe, define, or provide extra information about it. They are set off by commas.* Display the appositive found in the text. Annotate as you explain: *Thomas Edison is the first noun we see in this sentence. Notice the comma that comes after his name. The next part of the sentence, "one of the most famous inventors of all time," provides more information about Thomas Edison. It starts and ends with a comma. This is the appositive. Notice the comma that ends the appositive.* Show the appositive text in Spanish. Ask students to compare and contrast the English and Spanish text to recognize the structure of appositives in each language. *What do you observe?* *What do you notice?* Explain that in each language, the first noun phrase names a person or a subject. Then, after a comma, the second phrase describes, defines, or provides more information about the subject. In English, the second comma separates the appositive from the predicate of the sentence.	An appositive is a noun phrase that comes before another noun phrase to describe, define, or provide more information about it. Use commas to separate noun phrases. **Thomas Edison**, one of the most famous inventors of all time, invented the phonograph. **Lo inventó Thomas Edison**, uno de los inventores más famosos de todos los tiempos.

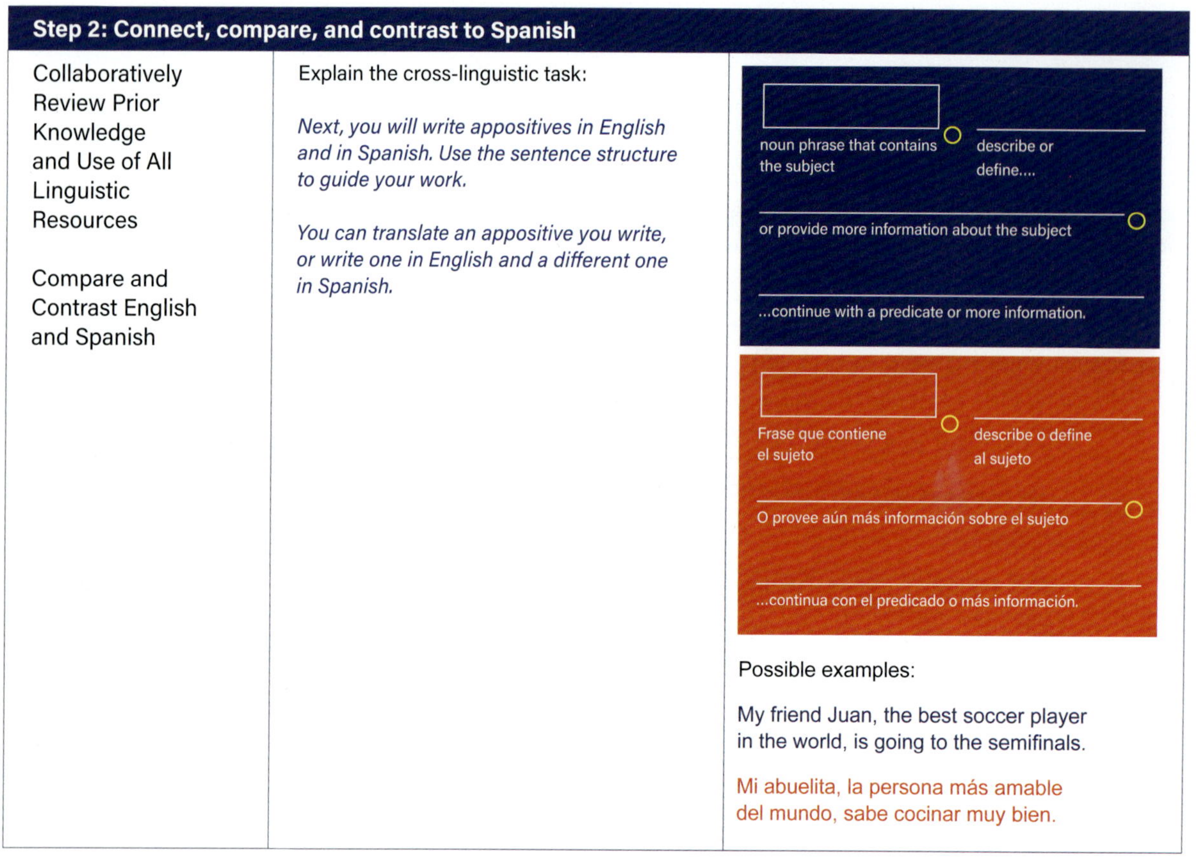

Step 2: Connect, compare, and contrast to Spanish		
Collaboratively Review Prior Knowledge and Use of All Linguistic Resources Compare and Contrast English and Spanish	Explain the cross-linguistic task: *Next, you will write appositives in English and in Spanish. Use the sentence structure to guide your work.* *You can translate an appositive you write, or write one in English and a different one in Spanish.*	noun phrase that contains the subject / describe or define.... / or provide more information about the subject / ...continue with a predicate or more information. Frase que contiene el sujeto / describe o define al sujeto / O provee aún más información sobre el sujeto / ...continua con el predicado o más información. Possible examples: My friend Juan, the best soccer player in the world, is going to the semifinals. Mi abuelita, la persona más amable del mundo, sabe cocinar muy bien.

> "When students are literate in one language, they can use their understanding of syntactic structures as a foundation for learning and mastering the syntax of a second language."

Step 3: Promote metalinguistic skills by summarizing the learning	
Affirm Biliteracy and Language Connections	*Appositives help clarify, define, and provide additional information to the noun they modify. In both English and in Spanish, appositives help writers be more precise by providing specific information and key details. Understanding and using appositives effectively in two languages improves reading and writing skills.*
Summarize What Was Learned	*What did we learn about appositives in English?* *Why is it important to understand appositives in English and Spanish?*

Teaching grammar and syntax is critical for language development.

Assessment Considerations

Grammar and syntax are a key components of language proficiency assessments in both English and Spanish Language Arts. A practical way to assess students for evidence of cross-linguistic transfer as it relates to grammar and syntax is by analyzing a constructed response in each language.

For example, students in the Spanish class are asked to write a paragraph to describe an animal of their choice. The prompt emphasizes the use of adjectives and prepositional phrases.

Escribe un párrafo que describa tu animal favorito. Asegúrate de usar varios adjetivos y frases preposicionales para que el lector entienda lo que estás describiendo y por qué te gusta.

In the English class, students are asked to write a descriptive paragraph of a room in their homes. Again, the prompt emphasizes the use of adjectives and prepositional phrases.

Write a paragraph that describes your favorite room in your house. Be sure to use many adjectives and prepositional phrases so the reader understands what you are describing and why you like it.

Teachers then compare students' writing to evaluate the general understanding of adjectives and prepositional phrases to describe and the specific rules that apply to the two grammatical constructs in each language.

Other Essential Factors

There are some essential factors to consider when assessing grammar/syntax in a bilingual instructional context to ensure a comprehensive understanding of student performance.

- **Language Dominance:** Be aware of the student's language dominance as this naturally affects their syntactic and grammatical understanding. Some students may demonstrate stronger syntax skills in Spanish, while others may excel in English. Teachers highlight a student's strengths in one language and use their awareness as a bridge to understand how the same syntactic and grammatical concepts work in the other language.
- **Cross-Linguistic Interferences:** As students learn a new language, they overgeneralize and use what they successfully apply in their dominant language to their new language. These overgeneralizations can often lead to deviations from "standard language" use. Such "errors" represent students' good faith approximations and attempts to express themselves in their new language.

By considering these factors, teachers can conduct more valid and meaningful assessments of students' grammatical and syntactic abilities and plan for instructional next steps tailored to students' linguistic understanding of the same concepts across languages.

Pause and Reflect

What two strategies from this chapter would you like to implement or enhance in your instruction?

Why is it important to teach grammar and syntax explicitly?

Conclusion

This chapter underscored the critical role of grammar and syntax in language acquisition and biliteracy. By understanding the principles of grammar and syntax, learners can effectively navigate between languages and express themselves clearly and cohesively. Moreover, the comparison between English and Spanish grammar and syntax serves to enhance linguistic awareness and proficiency in both languages. Using parallel language frames and parallel texts, educators can provide structured support to learners, fostering cross-linguistic understanding and academic success.

The use of brief constructed responses is a helpful strategy for assessing grammar and syntax. When doing so, it is critical to understand students' language dominance and recognize cross-linguistic interferences. This allows for tailored instruction and meaningful assessment of grammatical and syntactic abilities across languages.

Constructed writing responses are helpful for assessing grammar and syntax.

Key Takeaways

Grammar and syntax are the language frameworks that allow speakers and writers to convey their ideas clearly and accurately.

While they have these two language subsystems in common, Spanish and English each have specific grammatical rules and syntactical patterns.

Biliteracy requires cognitive flexibility that allows individuals to switch between two languages seamlessly. Understanding how language works through grammar and syntax accelerates the development of biliteracy.

It cannot be assumed that students will understand and effectively transfer a grammatical construct from one language to the other. Explicit cross-linguistic transfer instruction is key.

Analyzing sentence types, sentence frames, and response frames side-by-side enables students to gain proficient use of these language structures across languages.

Using parallel texts and parallel text structures is an efficient way to plan cross-linguistic lessons through each of the language subsystems across languages.

Analysis of student writing is an effective and practical way to assess students for evidence of cross-linguistic transfer relating to grammar and syntax.

Chapter 10

Pragmatics

> "A través de la educación multicultural, capacitamos a los estudiantes para convertirse en ciudadanos globales que abrazan y respetan las diferencias culturales, fomentando la paz y la armonía en nuestro mundo. La verdadera belleza del multiculturalismo reside en su capacidad para unir divisiones, fomentar la empatía y crear un sentimiento de pertenencia para todos".
>
> *"Through multicultural education, we empower students to become global citizens who embrace and respect cultural differences, fostering peace and harmony in our world. The true beauty of multiculturalism lies in its ability to bridge divides, foster empathy, and create a sense of belonging for all."*
>
> –Ada & Campoy, 2023a

This chapter addresses pragmatics as one of the language subsystems and emphasizes its importance in language study. Pragmatics is the study of how language is used in real-world contexts. It considers factors such as context, social dynamics, and speaker intentions to convey meaning beyond literal interpretations. Pragmatics is especially important to consider in bilingual and bicultural settings as individuals navigate between different cultural frameworks and communication styles. The importance of context in interpreting meaning is highlighted throughout this chapter, including physical setting, speaker identity, shared knowledge, and cultural norms. Cross-linguistic strategies and lessons are also shared, along with several methods for assessing pragmatics. This chapter provides a comprehensive understanding of pragmatics and its implications for language learning, cross-cultural communication, and biliteracy.

In This Chapter

Pragmatics

Pragmatics is a vital aspect of language study. It focuses on how language is used in real-world contexts to convey meaning beyond the literal interpretations of words and sentences. It deals with the ways in which context, social factors, and speaker intentions influence communication. As a language subsystem, pragmatics examines the rules and conventions that govern effective communication within a particular language community.

Language can serve various basic functions such as expressing needs, making requests, giving commands, asking questions, and making promises. For example, asking "Could you please pass the salt?" is not just a question about salt, it is expressing a need and a request.

Pragmatics also involves the importance of context in interpreting meaning. This context can include the physical setting, the identities and relationships of the speakers, shared knowledge, cultural norms, and the ongoing conversation. For example, the meaning of the phrase "I'll think about it" could signify genuine consideration in one context, while in another it may be a polite way of saying "no" without directly declining.

Three important dimensions of pragmatics are implications, assumptions, and politeness. Implication involves conveying meaning indirectly. Speakers often imply information rather than explicitly stating it, relying on shared understanding and contextual cues. For instance, if someone says "There are cookies in the staff lounge," this may imply that it's okay for staff members to eat these cookies.

Assumptions are presuppositions that speakers make about the shared knowledge or beliefs of their audience. Speakers often structure their speech based on these assumptions. For example, saying "Have you stopped drinking coffee?" presupposes that the person being addressed was previously drinking coffee.

Finally, courtesy language or politeness is used to maintain social harmony. To avoid causing offense or conflict, speakers employ various strategies, such as using indirect speech, employing honorifics, and mitigating requests.

Most important of all, pragmatics acknowledges that language behaviors and norms can vary across different cultures and communities. What may be considered appropriate or polite in one culture could be perceived differently in another. What can be assumed or presupposed in one culture may be completely opposite in another.

In *Guiding Principles of Dual Language Education* (2018) Howard and colleagues affirm cross-cultural competence as a pillar of dual-language education. Pragmatics is about understanding the intricacies of language use in everyday communication—and how competent speakers navigate the complexities of social interaction through language. It is a crucial subsystem of language study as it sheds light on how meaning is constructed and conveyed beyond the literal interpretation of words and grammar. The dynamics of cross-cultural competence is embedded in pragmatics.

> "Pragmatics...focuses on how language is used in real-world contexts to convey meaning beyond the literal interpretations of words and sentences."

Learn More

Ducuara, J. J., & Rozo, H. A. (2018). Biliteracy: A systematic literature review about strategies to teach and learn two languages. *Theory and Practice in Language Studies, 8*(10), 1307–1318.

Butvilofsky, S., Escamilla, K., & Hopewell, S. (2023). *Biliterate writing from the start: The literacy squared approach to asset-based writing instruction.* Brookes Publishing.

Pragmatics and Biliteracy

Pragmatics plays a significant role in understanding how bilingualism and biculturalism intersect. In the process of becoming bilingual and bicultural, individuals navigate between multiple cultural frameworks, each with its own set of "pragmatic norms" and communication styles. Understanding cultural pragmatics—the implicit rules and conventions governing communication within a culture—is essential for bicultural individuals to navigate social interactions effectively.

Bilingualism and biculturalism involve complex processes of identity negotiation, where individuals navigate multiple linguistic and cultural identities. Language pragmatics plays a role in shaping how individuals express their identity, establish rapport with others, and negotiate their belonging within different linguistic and cultural communities. Bilingual individuals may strategically adapt their pragmatic behavior to align with specific cultural norms or social expectations, depending on the context. Bicultural individuals may draw on their knowledge of both cultures to adapt their communication style and negotiate their identity within different social contexts.

Key Terms

Implications: Information conveyed indirectly without explicitly stating it.

Assumptions: Presuppositions that speakers make about the shared knowledge or beliefs of their audience.

Politeness: Courtesy language used to maintain social harmony.

Politeness strategies vary across cultures and languages, influencing the way individuals express courtesy, respect, and social hierarchy in communication. Bilingual-bicultural individuals may employ different politeness strategies depending on the language and cultural context of the interaction. Understanding the pragmatic nuances of politeness is crucial for bilingual individuals so they can navigate social interactions smoothly in both linguistic and cultural settings.

Understanding the pragmatic aspects of language use is essential for bilingual and bicultural individuals seeking to communicate effectively, negotiate their identity, and navigate their social worlds across languages. Respecting cultural differences is essential for effective cross-cultural communication and building positive interpersonal relationships in diverse contexts.

Caveat

Certain pragmatic norms or speech acts may be more prevalent in one language and culture than another, leading to pragmatic interference. For example, nonverbal communication, including gestures, facial expressions, and body language, varies across cultures and can convey different meanings.

Emerging bilingual-bicultural individuals may mistakenly use pragmatic strategies or norms from one language and try to apply them to the other. Because these norms often vary from one culture to another, a direct transfer is not always possible. For example, cultural norms around personal space and physical proximity influence interpersonal interactions. Some cultures prefer closer physical proximity during conversations, while others maintain greater distance. Understanding these differences is crucial for effective cross-cultural communication.

Other cultural, linguistic, and pragmatic factors that impact communication across languages include:

Turn-Taking and Interrupting: Cultures differ in their expectations regarding turn-taking in conversations and the acceptability of interrupting. In some cultures, such as those in Western societies, individuals often take turns speaking and may interrupt to express agreement or disagreement, while in others, listening without interruption is valued.

Conflict Resolution: Cultural norms influence approaches to conflict resolution and negotiation. Some cultures prioritize direct confrontation and resolution of conflicts, while others may avoid conflict or seek harmony through indirect communication strategies.

Hierarchy and Authority: Cultural hierarchies and power dynamics affect communication styles and interactions. In hierarchical cultures, individuals may show deference to authority figures and use formal language registers, while in more egalitarian cultures, communication may be more informal.

Cross-Linguistic Connections

Several scholars and researchers have written about various aspects of cultural parameters, contributing to our understanding of how culture shapes human behavior, social interactions, and identity. Edward T. Hall (1966) introduced the concept of "proxemics" in his book *The Hidden Dimension*, where he discusses the role of space and how people use space to communicate. Others, like Gary Weaver (2013), use an iceberg analogy for intercultural relations to illustrate the complexities of culture. Like an iceberg, much of culture is unseen, below the surface. The visible aspects of culture, above the waterline, represent observable categories, such as language, clothing, and food. These aspects are easily noticed and are often the focus of cultural stereotypes. However, below the surface lies the bulk of culture, the invisible and deeper elements that shape behaviors. These include values, beliefs, norms, and worldview. These aspects are often implicit and not immediately apparent to outsiders. Yet they play a crucial role in shaping how individuals and societies function.

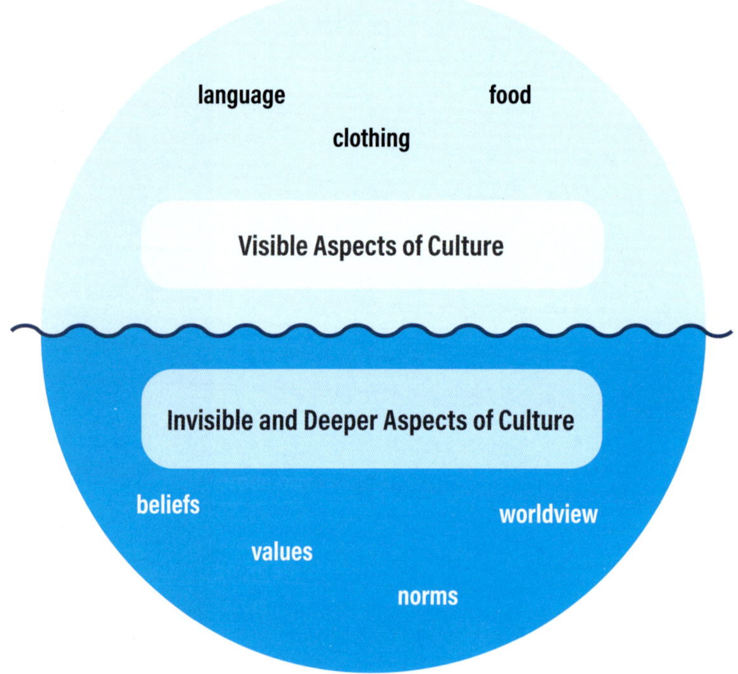

Culture encompasses a broad range of parameters that collectively shape the beliefs, values, practices, norms, and behaviors of a particular group of people. These parameters are interconnected and dynamic, reflecting the complex and multifaceted nature of all human cultures. Nelson Brooks (1968) describes twenty-five parameters of culture. He emphasized the importance of culture for language learning. Some of the key parameters of culture include the ones shown in this table. This is not an all inclusive list, but it highlights the most important parameters that are relevant to K–12 instruction.

Cultural Parameters

Parameter	Definition
Language	Language is a central aspect of culture, serving as a primary means of communication and expression within a community. It shapes thought patterns, social interactions, and cultural identity, influencing how individuals perceive and interpret the world around them. There are different registers of language: formal register, such as language used in academics, official documents, and ceremonies. Neutral register, language used in everyday communication, is generally clear and respectful, but not formal. Informal register, used in casual or familiar settings such as conversations with family and close friends, may not strictly adhere to grammatical rules or standard usage.
Beliefs and Values	Beliefs and values encompass the guiding principles, ideologies, and moral codes shared by members of a culture. They shape individuals' attitudes, priorities, and decision-making processes, influencing social norms and behaviors within the community.
Customs and Traditions	Customs and traditions refer to the rituals, ceremonies, practices, and behaviors passed down through generations within a culture. They play a significant role in social cohesion, identity formation, and cultural continuity, providing a sense of belonging and shared heritage.
Social Organization	Social organization encompasses the structure and dynamics of relationships within a society, including family structures, kinship systems, social roles, and hierarchies. It defines patterns of interaction, distribution of power, and social obligations between individuals and groups.
Art, Literature, and Aesthetics	Art, literature, and aesthetics encompass the creative expressions, artistic forms, and cultural artifacts produced by a society. They reflect cultural values, historical narratives, and aesthetic preferences, serving as vehicles for cultural expression, identity assertion, and collective memory.
Cultural Norms and Etiquette	Cultural norms and etiquette encompass the unwritten rules, conventions, and expectations governing social behavior and interaction within a culture. They dictate appropriate conduct, communication styles, and social etiquette in various contexts, facilitating social cohesion.
Religion and Spirituality	Religion and spirituality encompass the beliefs, rituals, practices, and sacred texts that provide meaning, purpose, and moral guidance to individuals within a culture. They influence worldview, ethics, and social institutions, shaping cultural identity and community cohesion.
Cultural Symbols and Icons	Cultural symbols and icons encompass the tangible and intangible representations of a culture's identity, values, and heritage. They include flags, emblems, landmarks, myths, heroes, and other symbolic artifacts that evoke both shared meanings and collective identity.
Technology and Resources	Technology and resources encompass the tools, artifacts, and material resources produced and utilized by a culture. They reflect technological advancements, economic systems, and lifestyle practices, shaping everyday life and cultural practices.
Cultural Geography and Environment	Cultural geography and environment encompass the geographical context, ecological conditions, and natural resources that influence cultural practices and adaptation strategies within a society. They shape settlement patterns, subsistence strategies, and cultural landscapes.

(Brooks, 1968)

These parameters evolve over time through interactions with internal and external influences across cultures. They contribute to the richness, diversity, and complexity of human societies, shaping individuals' identities, behaviors, experiences, and language. Educators who are familiar with these parameters can highlight them as they teach content knowledge as well as literature by asking students to consider how they impact the cultural and linguistic perspectives of diverse groups of people.

Social Interactions

Language and culture play a crucial role in social interactions, influencing the dynamics, outcomes, and perceptions within interpersonal communication. The charts that follow give examples of social interactions and explain how to intentionally connect, compare, and contrast these types of interactions across languages.

It is best to use examples drawn from literature, content knowledge, or students' existing funds of knowledge. Use questions and discussion prompts to invite students to notice cultural and linguistic nuances, implications, and assumptions. The teacher asks students to think about assumptions and implications of the language use in each language. Prompts in each language are slightly different so that these various aspects can be studied in each language while avoiding redundancy.

Pragmatics includes social dynamics and interactions.

Greetings and Courtesies	Saludos y cortesías
Description The way people greet each other varies across cultures and social contexts. Language dictates the choice of words, tone, and gestures used in greetings, which can convey respect, warmth, familiarity, or formality.	**Descripción** La forma de saludarse varía según la cultura y el contexto social. El lenguaje dicta la elección de las palabras, el tono y los gestos utilizados en los saludos, que pueden transmitir respeto, calidez, familiaridad o formalidad.
Instructional Strategy Invite students to act out the different greetings. Notice the different registers. *How do we use language to show our respect? Do we greet everyone in the same way?*	**Estrategia de enseñanza** Invite a los estudiantes a actuar los diferentes saludos. Observen los diferentes registros. *¿Cómo usamos el lenguaje para demostrar nuestro respeto? ¿Saludamos a todos de la misma manera?*
Formal Greetings ▪ It is a pleasure to meet you. ▪ Nice to meet you. ▪ How do you do? ▪ Have a nice day! ▪ Excuse me. ▪ Pardon me. **Informal Greetings** ▪ Howdy! ▪ What's up? ▪ What's happening? ▪ See ya later. ▪ Take care. ▪ Sorry folks! ▪ Oops, my bad!	**Saludos formales** ▪ Es un placer conocerle. ▪ Encantado de conocerle. ▪ ¿Cómo está usted? ▪ Tenga un buen día. ▪ Con permiso. ▪ Disculpe. **Saludos informales** ▪ Hola. ▪ ¿Qué tal? ▪ ¿Qué pasa? ▪ Nos vemos luego. ▪ Cuídate. ▪ Lo siento amigos. ▪ ¡Qué pena! Mi culpa.

Conversation Dynamics	Dinámica de conversación
Description Language shapes conversational dynamics, including turn-taking, topic maintenance, and the balance between speaking and listening. Politeness strategies, such as using indirect speech acts or hedging, can influence the flow and tone of conversations.	**Descripción** El lenguaje determina la dinámica de la conversación, los turnos, el mantenimiento de los temas y el equilibrio entre hablar y escuchar. Las estrategias de cortesía, como los actos de habla indirectos o las evasivas, pueden influir en la fluidez y el tono de las conversaciones.
Instructional Strategy *Let's connect, compare, and contrast the language we use during our academic conversations.* *Why is it important to know these conversation moves in English and in Spanish?* *How do we use language strategically to succeed during academic or personal conversations?*	**Estrategia de enseñanza** *Conectemos, comparemos y contrastemos el lenguaje que utilizamos durante nuestras conversaciones académicas. ¿Por qué es importante conocer estrategias para las conversaciones en inglés y en español?* *¿Cómo usamos el lenguaje estratégicamente para tener éxito durante las conversaciones académicas o personales?*
▪ I agree with you because _____. ▪ I have a question about _____. ▪ Based on the text, I think that _____. ▪ Based on my experience, I know that _____. ▪ Please explain what you mean by _____. ▪ I would like to add that _____.	▪ Estoy de acuerdo contigo porque _____. ▪ Tengo una pregunta sobre _____. ▪ Basándome en el texto, creo que _____. ▪ Basándome en mi experiencia, sé que _____. ▪ Explica qué quieres decir con _____. ▪ Me gustaría añadir que _____.

Negotiation and Persuasion	Negociación y persuasión
Description Language is instrumental in negotiating agreements, resolving conflicts, and persuading others to adopt certain viewpoints or behaviors. Effective negotiation skills involve using language strategically to convey arguments, offer concessions, and reach mutually beneficial outcomes.	**Descripción** El lenguaje es fundamental para negociar acuerdos, resolver conflictos y persuadir a los demás para que adopten determinados puntos de vista o comportamientos. Para negociar con eficacia hay que utilizar el lenguaje de forma estratégica para transmitir argumentos, ofrecer concesiones y alcanzar resultados beneficiosos para ambas partes.
Instructional Strategy *What are key phrases that may be used to acknowledge others' points of view while disagreeing? When and where would you use this language?*	**Estrategia de enseñanza** *¿Cuáles son las frases clave que pueden utilizarse para reconocer los puntos de vista de los demás al tiempo que se discrepa? ¿Cuándo y dónde utilizarías este lenguaje?* *¿Por qué es importante reconocer las perspectivas de los demás? ¿Qué notas igual en ambos lenguajes?*
▪ I understand your perspective, however _____. ▪ While I respect your opinion, I must disagree because _____. ▪ While I value your input, I have a different perspective on this _____.	▪ Entiendo tu perspectiva, sin embargo _____. ▪ Aunque valoro tu opinión, tengo que ofrecerte un punto de vista diferente _____. ▪ Puedo apreciar tu perspectiva, aunque tengo un punto de vista diferente _____.

Social Hierarchies and Power Dynamics	Jerarquías sociales y dinámicas de poder
Description Language reflects and reinforces social hierarchies and power dynamics within interactions. Formal language registers, titles, and deferential speech patterns are used to show respect to those in positions of authority or higher social status.	**Descripción** El lenguaje refleja y refuerza las jerarquías sociales y las dinámicas de poder en las interacciones. Los registros lingüísticos formales, los títulos y los patrones de habla deferentes se utilizan para mostrar respeto a quienes ocupan posiciones de autoridad o tienen un estatus social más elevado.
Instructional Strategy *How does language reflect respect?* *Why is it important to use language to demonstrate respect? Compare and contrast the English and Spanish phrases.* *Showing respect during conversations or with someone in authority or with an older person is important for personal and social success. Where, when, and with whom would you use these phrases?*	**Estrategia de enseñanza** *¿Cómo es que el lenguaje refleja respeto?* *¿Por qué es importante utilizar el lenguaje para demostrar respeto? Compara y contrasta frases en español y en inglés.* *El demostrar respeto durante las conversaciones o con alguien de autoridad o con una persona mayor es importante para el éxito personal y social. ¿Dónde, cuándo y con quién usarías estas frases?*
▪ Please. ▪ Thank you. ▪ Excuse me. ▪ I value your ideas. ▪ I respect your opinions. ▪ I am grateful to you for _____.	▪ Por favor. ▪ Gracias. ▪ Con permiso. ▪ Valoro sus ideas. ▪ Respeto sus opiniones.* ▪ Estoy agradecido por lo que usted _____. * Se usan los pronombres su y usted para indicar formalidad.

Expressing Emotions and Empathy	Expresión de emociones y empatía
Description Language enables individual expression and understanding. Language enables individuals to express and interpret emotions, fostering empathy and connection in social interactions. Through verbal and nonverbal cues, people convey feelings such as joy, sadness, anger, and empathy, which contribute to building rapport and understanding.	**Descripción** El lenguaje permite expresión propia y comprensión. El lenguaje permite a las personas expresar e interpretar emociones, fomentando la empatía y la conexión en las interacciones sociales. A través de señales verbales y no verbales, las personas transmiten sentimientos como la alegría, la tristeza, la ira y la empatía, que contribuyen a crear compenetración y comprensión.
Instructional Strategy *How do expressing emotions and empathy help when making connections with others?* *What similarities or differences do you notice as you analyze the English and Spanish phrases?* *Why is it beneficial to know how to express emotions and empathy in more than one language? Do you notice any difference between English and Spanish phrases?*	**Estrategia de enseñanza** *¿Cómo ayudan la expresión de emociones y la empatía a establecer conexiones con los demás? ¿Qué similitudes o diferencias observas al analizar las frases en español y en inglés?* *¿Por qué es beneficioso saber expresar emociones y empatía en más de un idioma? ¿Notas alguna diferencia entre las frases en inglés y en español?*
• How are you, how are you doing? • Is there something I can do to help? • I am here to support you. • I care about you. • I care about how you feel. • I am sorry to hear that. • I understand.	• ¿Cómo estás? ¿Cómo te sientes? • ¿Hay algo que puedo hacer para ayudarte? • Estoy aquí para apoyarte. • Me importas mucho. • Me importa cómo te sientes. • Lamento escuchar esto. • Te comprendo.

Sayings and Proverbs	Refranes y proverbios
Description Sayings and proverbs are short, traditional expressions that convey wisdom, advice, or cultural insights. They are often passed down through generations within a particular culture or community and are used to teach lessons, offer guidance, or comment on human behavior and experiences.	**Descripción** Los refranes y proverbios son expresiones breves y tradicionales que transmiten sabiduría, consejos o conocimientos culturales. Suelen transmitirse de generación en generación dentro de una cultura o comunidad determinada y se utilizan para enseñar lecciones, ofrecer orientación o comentar el comportamiento y las experiencias humanas.
Instructional Strategy *Have you heard any of these saying or proverbs?* *Who were you with and when did you first heard it?* *What values are expressed that are the same or similar in English and Spanish?*	**Estrategia de enseñanza** *¿Has escuchado alguno de estos proverbios o refranes? ¿Con quién estabas y cuando lo escuchaste? ¿Cuáles de estos refranes dan un consejo similar en inglés y en español?*
• Better late than never. • An ounce of prevention is worth a pound of cure. • Tell me who you walk with, and I will tell you who you are. • Silence is golden. • Every cloud has a silver lining. • Don't put off until tomorrow what you can do today.	• Más vale tarde que nunca. • Más vale prevenir que lamentar. • Dime con quién andas y te diré quién eres. • Ojos que no ven, corazón que no siente. • En boca cerrada no entran moscas. • No hay mal que por bien no venga. • No dejes para mañana lo que puedes hacer hoy.

Cultural Norms and Identity Expression	Normas culturales y expresión de identidad
Description Language reflects cultural norms and values, shaping how individuals express their identity and belonging within social groups. Slang, dialects, code-switching, and idioms are examples of linguistic practices that signal group membership and cultural identity.	**Descripción** El lenguaje refleja normas y valores culturales y determina la forma en que los individuos expresan su identidad y su pertenencia a un grupo social. La jerga, los dialectos y los cambios de código son ejemplos de prácticas lingüísticas que señalan la pertenencia a un grupo y la identidad cultural.
Instructional Strategy *What do you think about code-switching between Spanish and English?* *Connect, compare, and contrast the code-switched sentences.* *Why do you think it is beneficial or advantageous to understand slang phrases and idioms in both English and Spanish?*	**Estrategia de enseñanza** *¿Qué piensas sobre los cambios de código entre el español y el inglés? Conecta, compara y contrasta las frases con cambios de códigos.* *¿Por qué crees que es beneficioso o ventajoso entender frases hechas y modismos tanto en inglés como en español?*
Idioms • Piece of cake. • He is on cloud 9. • Spill the beans. • Hit the road. • Hang out and chill out. • It costs an arm and a leg. • Don't get FOMO. • He is the black sheep.	**Expresiones idiomáticas** • Pan comido. • Está en las nubes. • Cuesta un ojo de la cara. • Está como una cabra. • Está en las últimas. • Echar agua al mar. • Ponte las pilas. • Es la oveja negra.
Code-Switching Examples • I am going to *la tienda* with *mi primo*. • The *maestra* said to clean out *los* desks.	**Ejemplos de cambios de código** • Dame el *pencil* para terminar mi *work*. • *Hurry-up* y come que vas a llegar *late*.

Social Media and Online Communication	**Redes sociales y comunicación en línea**
Description In the digital age, language is central to online interactions through social media platforms, messaging apps, and virtual communities. The use of emojis, hashtags, and memes adds layers of meaning and facilitates connection in digital social spaces.	**Descripción** En la era digital, el lenguaje es fundamental en las interacciones en línea a través de plataformas de redes sociales, aplicaciones de mensajería y comunidades virtuales. El uso de emojis, hashtags y memes añade capas de significado y facilita la conexión en los espacios sociales digitales.
Instructional Strategy *How is knowing two languages an advantage when it comes to social and online communication?* *What do you notice about the technology terms used in English and in Spanish? Create a media term glossary.* *Do you use social networks to communicate in Spanish and English?* *How do you think emojis and visual symbols contribute to communication between different languages? Design a new symbol or emoji.*	**Estrategia de enseñanza** *¿De qué manera el conocimiento de otros idiomas supone una ventaja para la comunicación social y en línea? ¿Qué observas en los términos tecnológicos utilizados en inglés y en español? Crea un glosario de términos relacionados con los medios de comunicación.* *¿Usas las redes sociales para comunicarte en español y en inglés? ¿Cómo piensas que los emojis y los símbolos visuales contribuyen a la comunicación entre diferentes idiomas? Diseña un símbolo o emoji nuevo.*
• Hashtag • Like • Share • Retweet • Post • Notification • Influencer • Follower • Emoji	• Etiqueta • Me gusta • Compartir • Retuitear • Publicar • Notificación • Influenciador • Seguidor • Emoji

As seen in the previous tables' examples, interpersonal communication is both complex and nuanced, especially when we consider it in a bilingual context. Language serves as a multifaceted tool for navigating social interactions, shaping interpersonal relationships, and constructing social reality within diverse cultural contexts.

Pragmatics and Writing

Pragmatics plays a crucial role in writing by influencing how writers convey meaning, establish rapport with readers, and achieve their communicative goals. Here are several ways in which pragmatics relates to writing and how teachers can incorporate cross-cultural awareness in writing assignments and writing prompts.

Audience Awareness

- In both English and Spanish, audience awareness emphasizes the importance of considering the audience's background, expectations, and cultural norms when crafting written texts. Teachers alert writers to use their cultural and linguistic knowledge to anticipate how their audience will interpret their words and adjust their writing style, tone, and content accordingly to engage their specific audience effectively.

Politeness and Tone

- Pragmatics also informs decisions about politeness strategies and tone in writing. Teachers guide students by having them choose language and expressions that align with the desired level of formality, respectfulness, or familiarity appropriate for the intended audience and purpose of the text. Students can consider using politeness markers such as please, thank you, and expressions of deference. These can enhance rapport with the reader and convey respect.

Adaptation to Medium

- Pragmatics also considers how the medium of communication influences writing strategies and conventions. Teachers point out to students that writing style must be adapted and formatting choices should suit different mediums—such as print, digital platforms, or social media—while also considering cultural factors such as audience engagement, readability, and interactivity.

Understanding the dynamics of pragmatics provides valuable insights into the communicative strategies and considerations involved in writing—guiding writers in crafting texts that effectively engage readers, convey meaning, and achieve their communicative goals within the diverse linguistic and cultural background of the intended readers.

Writing styles need to adapt to the medium used for communication.

 |

Writing Instruction in a Biliteracy Context

Ideation and organization of thinking, as well as the writing process, are general transfer skills; therefore, they are the same for English and Spanish. However, the syntax and grammar conventions applied in writing are specific to each language. For example, when writing narrative, informative, or opinion essays, students undergo the same mental process in both languages, use the same organizational skills, and adhere to the same characteristics of the writing type. While teaching writing, teachers emphasize text-type characteristics, text structures, and transition words, using similar anchor charts and graphic organizers for each language. The written outcome, however, is specific to the language that the text is written in and must adhere to its language rules. Cross-linguistic transfer in writing is achieved across languages through similarity of learning conditions.

It is recommended that teachers focus on the same writing type (narrative, informative, opinion) simultaneously in both languages because transfer is achieved through similarity of learning conditions. In other words, during a unit, students learn and focus on the characteristics of the same writing type in each language. In doing so, they are able to maximize their understanding of genre characteristics, text structures, transition words, and text organization in each language.

In both Spanish and English, teachers model and guide students explicitly while teaching the specific grammar and syntactical features that apply in reading and writing. The examples that follow present suggestions for allocating writing support in a biliteracy context. All options may be implemented in any writing type or genre.

Allocating Writing Support in a Biliteracy Context

Option	Allocation	Instructional Focus Example
1	Allocate writing process lessons in one language. Allocate constructed responses to the partner language that support the content knowledge of the writing.	**Genre** Students follow the writing process and learn the writing type and its characteristics in one language. For example: *Write an informative essay on a particular habitat.* Students write constructed responses relating to the same topic in the other language. For example: *According to the text, how do animals survive in a desert habitat?*
2	<u>Same reading text</u> in both languages, but students respond to <u>a different prompt</u> in each language.	**Text Reference** By analyzing the same text in two languages, students respond to different prompts in each language and develop text referencing skills across languages as they evaluate and interpret ideas when reading. For example, after reading the Aesop fable *The Lion and The Mouse*, they must respond to: Spanish prompt: *Si fueras el ratoncito, ¿que más le hubieras dicho al león para que te dejara libre?* English prompt: *You are the lion. Provide additional reasons for letting the mouse go free instead of eating it.*
3	<u>Different reading text</u> in each language and students respond to <u>a different prompt</u> in each language.	**Content Knowledge** As students reference and convey information in writing about related topics within a unit in two languages, they develop and increase their content-area knowledge and vocabulary—as they select, organize, and express ideas in each language. For example: while exploring how Earth changes over time, the Spanish text relates to volcanoes and the English text relates to earthquakes. Spanish prompt: *Explica cómo se forman los volcanes.* English prompt: *Explain how an earthquake happens.*
4	<u>Different text read</u> in each language, but students respond to <u>the same prompt</u> in each language.	**Author's Craft** When students analyze the language and techniques used by authors, they are motivated to adapt their own language choices when writing. They notice how meaning and cultural nuances are conveyed in each language. For example: after reading Alma Flor Ada's *Ser como Tú* (2023) in Spanish and Campoy and Howell's *Maybe Something Beautiful* (2016) in English, students must respond to: Spanish prompt: *¿De qué manera Alma Flor Ada usa los símiles en* Ser como tú*? Provee ejemplos.* English prompt: *How do Campoy and Howell use similes in* Maybe Something Beautiful*? Provide examples.*
5	<u>Same or different text.</u> Students write in one language and **<u>translate</u>** a sentence or paragraph to the partner language.	**Cross-Linguistic Analysis** Students employ their grammatical and syntactical awareness when translating their own writing from one language to another. Students avail themselves of what they know and have learned in one language and apply it to the other, resulting in deeper understanding of how language works in both languages. Students choose a piece of writing to translate into the other language.

In Action

Mr. Cervantes and Mrs. Torres are dual-language teachers who want to emphasize pragmatics in their Grade 6 classroom. They recognize the benefit of linguistic and cultural competence for their students and are always seeking ways to extend students' understanding of language beyond grammar and function.

Spanish to English Lesson: Using Registers

Mr. Cervantes wants to use role-play to teach language registers. By using simple drama strategies, he will engage students in various scenarios. A drama prompt will be assigned to a pair or triad of students. Students will then role-play to demonstrate how they can use and adapt their language resources according to social context in Spanish, then in English.

<table>
<tr><th colspan="3">Paso 1: Usar lo que ya sabemos y hemos aprendido sobre el español</th></tr>
<tr><td>Establecer el objetivo de la lección y la relación de transferencia</td><td>Hoy vamos a ver cómo podemos usar el lenguaje para interactuar apropiadamente para conversar en diferentes contextos sociales.</td><td rowspan="3"><table><tr><th>Tipo</th><th>Contexto</th><th>Ejemplo</th></tr><tr><td>Formal</td><td>Uso en contextos formales académicos, asuntos de gobierno, o con personas mayores.</td><td>Es un placer poder conversar con usted.</td></tr><tr><td>Informal</td><td>Uso en contextos informales en el hogar, con amigos y familiares.</td><td>¡Qué bueno que vamos a hablar juntas!</td></tr></table></td></tr>
<tr><td>Repasar la definición de registros de lenguaje</td><td>Ya sabemos que tanto en inglés como en español existen diferentes registros de lenguaje.</td></tr>
<tr><td>Confirmar el concepto de lo repasado y aprendido</td><td>Registro de lenguaje se refiere al nivel de formalidad en que se usa un lenguaje. Por ejemplo:
Registro formal – se usa en contextos académicos, asuntos de gobierno, o con personas mayores.

Registro informal – se usa entre amigos y familiares.

El nivel de formalidad con la que se usa un lenguaje de acuerdo con las normas culturales.</td></tr>
</table>

Paso 2: Conectar, comparar y contrastar con el inglés		
Preparación de manipulativos Colaboración y trabajo en pares o grupos Promover conocimientos previos y asociaciones Invitar a los estudiantes a compartir conocimientos con un compañero Afirmar la comparación y contraste entre ambos idiomas	*Vamos a formar grupos pequeños de 2 o 3 estudiantes para hacer una pequeña dramatización de acuerdo con una pauta.* Instrucciones: *Escojan la pauta que van a actuar.* *Lean la pauta.* *Preparen una breve escena.* *Cada persona tiene que hablar.* *Dramaticen la escena en español, y luego en inglés.* Los grupos toman turnos presentando sus escenas.	Ejemplos de pautas para la representación dramática: *Eres un maestro o maestra. Explícale el ciclo de vida de una mariposa a un estudiante de primer grado.* *Eres un científico. Dile a tu colega que no estás de acuerdo con su opinión sobre los cambios climáticos.* *Eres una mamá. Tu hija quiere ir al cine con su amiga. No estás de acuerdo.*

Paso 3: Promover destrezas metalingüísticas al resumir lo aprendido	
Resumir lo aprendido	*¿Qué hemos aprendido? ¿De qué manera cambia el lenguaje y entonación según las personas y el ambiente de la conversación? Tanto en inglés como en español existen los diferentes registros de lenguaje. Al hablar o conversar, usamos el lenguaje, tanto como las normas culturales para comunicarnos.*
Afirmar la lectoescritura bilingüe y las conexiones con el inglés	*Al hablar tanto en español como en inglés, tendremos más éxito en nuestras relaciones personales, en entornos académicos y en futuros ambientes de trabajo si somos conscientes de nuestro uso del idioma y de las normas culturales de quienes nos rodean.*

English to Spanish Lesson: Sayings and Proverbs

Mrs. Torres wants to emphasize how language carries cultural traditions, folklore, and wisdom that gets passed on from generation to generation in the form of sayings and proverbs. She recognizes that this is a great opportunity for meaningful parental involvement. She has students ask parents for any proverb or saying they remember or value. Some students have brought back their sayings in English while have brought back their sayings in Spanish. Mrs. Torres will ask students to share their sayings with a partner. She has also prepared a few correlating sayings in English and in Spanish. Students will analyze and pair the sayings according to the meaning they convey.

Step 1: Review what we know and have learned about English		
Introduce the Lesson Concept State the Lesson Objective State Transfer Relations Review Concepts Already Learned Model	*Today we are going to analyze sayings in English and in Spanish. In both English and Spanish, sayings are short, memorable phrases passed on from generation to generation that convey cultural wisdom and advice. While they can vary in the language used, some sayings convey similar values in a culture.* *For example, "Better late than never." This saying in English is conveying or expressing that doing something late is better than not doing it at all. In Spanish there is a similar saying: "Más vale tarde que nunca".* *While not a direct translation, it also conveys the advice that doing something late is better than not doing it at all. Having similar sayings in two distinct cultures is one way of recognizing common values across language and cultures.* *These two sayings express a common value that has been conveyed in different languages and existed across generations in two distinct cultures.*	Better late than never Más vale tarde que nunca

Step 2: Connect, compare, and contrast with Spanish		
Collaboration Work in Pairs or Small Groups Promote Prior Knowledge and Use of All Linguistic Resources Invite Students to Share with a Partner What They Have Learned Affirm the Transfer Relation by Stating Comparisons and Examples in English and Spanish	*Next, you will analyze a few sayings in English and Spanish.* *First, read each saying in each language.* *Then analyze the meaning and the cultural value, wisdom, or advice they convey.* *Next, match a saying in English with a saying in Spanish that has a similar message.* *Be ready to discuss with the whole class how you recognized the similar meanings and implications.*	Students pair English and Spanish sayings by similar meanings. Students receive them scrambled and must read and analyze them to pair them up. ▪ The early bird gets the worm. ▪ *Al que madruga, Dios lo ayuda.* ▪ Patience is a virtue. ▪ *La paciencia es la madre de todas las virtudes.* ▪ You reap what you sow. ▪ *El que siembra vientos, recoge tempestades.*

Step 3: Promote metalinguistic skills by summarizing the learning	
Summarize What Was Learned	*In both English and Spanish, sayings are short, memorable phrases passed on from generation to generation that convey cultural wisdom.* *Having similar sayings in two distinct cultures is one way of recognizing common values across language and cultures.*
Affirm Biliteracy and Language Connections	*Sayings and proverbs capture the insights and cultural wisdom of a culture.* *As we become bilingual and bicultural, we can recognize common ground between languages and cultures and attain multicultural proficiency that helps us interact successfully with others.*

Assessment Considerations for Pragmatics

Assessing pragmatics in the context of dual-language education involves evaluating students' ability to understand and use language appropriately within diverse cultural and linguistic contexts. The following are several strategies for assessing pragmatics in a dual-language context:

Observational Assessment Checklist

- Observational assessment involves observing students' interactions in naturalistic settings, such as classroom discussions, role-playing, group activities, or social interactions. Educators can observe students' use of language, politeness strategies, turn-taking behavior, and adherence to cultural norms to assess their pragmatic competence. The checklists on the following pages may be used by students and teachers to systematically observe, heighten awareness, and assess behaviors and attitudes related to cross-cultural awareness in various contexts.

Observation of students' adherence to cultural norms is helpful for assessing their awareness of bilingual bicultural pragmatics.

Observational Checklist for Cross-Cultural Awareness
Verbal Communication
☐ Demonstrates active listening skills ☐ Asks questions to clarify cultural nuances ☐ Uses respectful language without offensive remarks
Nonverbal Communication
☐ Maintains culturally appropriate eye contact ☐ Adapts body language and gestures to cultural norms ☐ Respects personal space boundaries across cultures
Empathy and Perspective-Taking
☐ Shows empathy toward individuals from different cultures ☐ Considers situations from multiple cultural perspectives ☐ Understands how cultural backgrounds influence behaviors
Cultural Sensitivity
☐ Recognizes own cultural biases and stereotypes ☐ Shows sensitivity toward cultural customs and traditions ☐ Demonstrates openness to learning about unfamiliar cultures
Conflict Resolution
☐ Handles conflicts with cultural sensitivity ☐ Resolves conflicts respectfully, considering cultural perspectives ☐ Negotiates mutually acceptable solutions across cultures
Collaboration and Teamwork
☐ Effectively collaborates with peers from diverse cultural backgrounds ☐ Navigates cultural differences within team settings ☐ Contributes to creating an inclusive learning environment
Cultural Knowledge and Awareness
☐ Demonstrates knowledge of different cultural practices and traditions ☐ Shows curiosity and engagement in learning about various cultures ☐ Recognizes and appreciates diversity within and across cultures
Self-Reflection and Growth
☐ Reflects on own cultural identity and its influence on interactions ☐ Open to feedback and willing to learn from experiences ☐ Commits to ongoing growth and development in cross-cultural competence

Developed by Silvia Dorta-Duque de Reyes

Lista de observaciones para la concientización intercultural

Comunicación verbal

- ☐ Demuestra capacidad de escuchar activamente
- ☐ Hace preguntas para aclarar matices culturales
- ☐ Utiliza un lenguaje respetuoso sin comentarios ofensivos

Comunicación no verbal

- ☐ Mantiene un contacto visual culturalmente apropiado
- ☐ Adapta el lenguaje corporal y los gestos a las normas culturales
- ☐ Respeta los límites del espacio personal de todas las culturas

Empatía y toma de perspectiva

- ☐ Muestra empatía hacia las personas de diferentes culturas
- ☐ Considera las situaciones desde múltiples perspectivas culturales
- ☐ Comprende cómo influyen los contextos culturales en los comportamientos

Sensibilidad cultural

- ☐ Reconoce sus propios prejuicios y estereotipos culturales
- ☐ Muestra sensibilidad hacia las costumbres y tradiciones culturales
- ☐ Demuestra receptividad al aprendizaje de culturas desconocidas

Resolución de conflictos

- ☐ Maneja los conflictos con sensibilidad cultural
- ☐ Resuelve conflictos respetuosamente, teniendo en cuenta las perspectivas culturales
- ☐ Negocia soluciones mutuamente aceptables entre grupos y entre culturas

Colaboración y trabajo en equipo

- ☐ Colabora eficazmente con compañeros de diversos orígenes culturales
- ☐ Maneja las diferencias culturales dentro de un equipo
- ☐ Contribuye a crear un entorno de aprendizaje integrador e inclusivo

Conocimiento y conciencia cultural

- ☐ Demuestra conocimiento de diferentes prácticas y tradiciones culturales
- ☐ Demuestra curiosidad y compromiso por aprender sobre diversas culturas
- ☐ Reconoce y aprecia la diversidad dentro de las culturas y entre ellas

Autorreflexión y crecimiento

- ☐ Reflexiona sobre su propia identidad cultural y su influencia en las interacciones
- ☐ Está abierto a la retroalimentación y dispuesto a aprender de las experiencias
- ☐ Se compromete a crecer y desarrollar continuamente la competencia intercultural

Desarrollado por Silvia Dorta-Duque de Reyes

> Assessing pragmatics in the context of dual-language education involves evaluating students' ability to understand and use language appropriately within diverse cultural and linguistic contexts.

Educators may want to focus on one or two areas of the checklist at a time, depending on the emphasis of a piece of literature or unit of study. This checklist can be adapted for student self-evaluation by starting the key indicator statements with "I can" and changing the initial verb to first-person form. For example:

Verbal Communication
☐ I can demonstrate active listening skills.
☐ I can ask questions to clarify cultural nuances.
☐ I can use respectful language without offensive remarks.

Comunicación verbal
☐ Puedo demostrar el escuchar activamente.
☐ Puedo hacer preguntas para aclarar matices culturales.
☐ Puedo utilizar un lenguaje respetuoso sin comentarios ofensivos.

Role-Play and Simulations

- Role-play activities and simulations provide opportunities for students to practice and demonstrate pragmatic skills in culturally and linguistically diverse scenarios. Educators can assess students' ability to adapt their language use, negotiate meaning, and navigate social interactions within different cultural contexts. Role-playing can be recorded to be included in digital portfolios. Students can provide a brief reflection of their learning.

Scenarios and Case Studies

- Presenting students with pragmatic scenarios or case studies allows educators to assess their understanding of cultural norms, social expectations, and appropriate language use. Students can analyze the context, identify relevant pragmatic features, and propose appropriate communication strategies to address the given situation. These scenarios can be drawn directly from texts studied in the classroom.

Assessment Considerations for Writing

Written assignments, such as essays, narratives, or reflections, can provide insights into students' pragmatic awareness and cultural sensitivity. Educators can assess students' ability to convey meaning effectively, consider audience expectations, and use appropriate language registers and politeness strategies in their written communication. Students may be asked to provide brief reflections, opinions, or personal narratives based on one of the parameters of culture as it relates to the essential understandings of a unit of knowledge currently implemented.

In *Biliteracy from the Start* (2014), Kathy Escamilla and her colleagues emphasize the importance of assessing student writing across languages side-by-side. This approach is rooted in the understanding that biliteracy development is a complex and multifaceted process that benefits from a holistic perspective.

By using a side-by-side assessment method, educators can collect both quantitative and qualitative evidence of students' writing in Spanish and English. This includes examining content, structural elements, spelling, and bilingual strategies at various levels such as discourse, sentence/phrase, word, and phonics. The cross-linguistic writing assessment charts that follow have been designed to facilitate the process of evaluating student writing across languages. Using these charts will help educators to discern and prioritize next instructional steps holistically as well as explicitly.

By employing a variety of assessment strategies differentiated to meet the linguistic needs of language learners in a dual-language context, educators can effectively evaluate students' pragmatic competence and provide targeted support to enhance their communicative skills within diverse cultural and linguistic contexts.

Cross-Linguistic Writing Assessment Analysis in a Dual-Language Context

Student's Name:	Date:	Writing Type:
English Notations	**Criteria**	**Spanish Notations**
	Adherence to Prompt Focus Development Coherence	
	Organization and Structure Text-Type Features Cohesion Condensing Ideas Connecting Ideas	
	Sentence Structure Word Order Literal Translations Code-Switching Sentence Variety	
	Grammar-Language Use Noun Phrases Verb Phrases Modifiers	
	Vocabulary Academic Content Specific Figurative High-Frequency Words	
	Spelling L1 Spelling Applied to L2 Absent Phonemes Phoneme Collapse Unfamiliar Pattern Word Boundaries L1 Substitutions	
	Punctuation Grade-Level Specific	
	Capitalization Grade-Level Specific	

NEXT INSTRUCTIONAL STEPS:

Análisis translingüístico para la evaluación de escritura en dos idiomas

Nombre del estudiante:	Fecha:	Tipo de Escritura:
Apuntes en español	**Criterio**	**Apuntes en inglés**
	Cumplimiento a la Pauta Enfoque Desarrollo Coherencia	
	Organización y Estructura Características del texto Cohesión Condensar ideas Conectar ideas	
	Estructura de Oraciones Orden de las palabras Tradiciones literales Cambio de códigos Variedad de oraciones	
	Gramática y uso del Lenguaje Frases sustantivas Frases verbales Modificadores	
	Vocabulario Académico De contenido específico Figurativo Palabras de uso frecuente	
	Ortografía Ortografía L1 aplicada al L2 Fonemas ausentes Colapso de fonemas Patrón de letras desconocido Contorno de las palabras Substituciones en L1	
	Puntuación específico al grado	
	Capitalización específico al grado	

PRÓXIMOS PASOS PARA LA INSTRUCCIÓN:

Pause and Reflect

How do the sample lessons look similar or different to the ways you've approached teaching pragmatics?

What are two understandings you took away from this chapter?

Conclusion

The study of pragmatics is a crucial pillar in language understanding and communication. By going beyond the literal interpretations of words and sentences, pragmatics illuminates the intricate ways in which language is wielded to convey meaning within real-world contexts. From the nuances of politeness strategies to the subtle implications and assumptions embedded in communication, pragmatics unveils the dynamic interplay between language, culture, and social dynamics.

In a world marked by linguistic diversity and cultural plurality, the insights gleaned from pragmatics become indispensable. Whether navigating cross-cultural interactions, fostering biliteracy and biculturalism, or honing communicative competence in diverse linguistic settings, an understanding of pragmatics equips individuals with the tools to bridge divides and foster understanding.

Educators play a pivotal role in nurturing communication skills and cultural sensitivity between learners. By incorporating pragmatic considerations into teaching practices and assessment strategies across languages, educators can empower students to navigate the complexities of language and culture with confidence and competence.

Ultimately, the study of pragmatics serves as a testament to the richness and complexity of human communication. By embracing its principles, we not only deepen our understanding of language, we also cultivate empathy, foster mutual respect, and pave the way for meaningful connections across linguistic and cultural boundaries.

Key Takeaways

Pragmatics is a vital aspect of language study, focusing on how language is used in real-world contexts to convey meaning beyond the literal interpretations of words.

Pragmatics also explores the importance of context in interpreting meaning.

In the process of becoming bilingual and bicultural, individuals navigate between multiple cultural and communicative contexts.

Bilingualism and biculturalism involve complex processes of identity negotiation, where individuals navigate multiple linguistic and cultural identities.

Culture encompasses a broad range of parameters that collectively shape the beliefs, values, practices, norms, and behaviors of a particular group of people.

Pragmatics plays a crucial role in writing by influencing how writers convey meaning, establish rapport with readers, and achieve their communicative goals.

By incorporating pragmatic considerations into teaching practices and assessment strategies across languages, educators can empower students to navigate the complexities of language and culture with confidence and competence.

Concluding Thoughts

Silvia Dorta-Duque de Reyes

Gentle Reader,

As you reach the conclusion of *The Dynamics of Cross-Linguistic Instruction*, I want to extend my heartfelt gratitude for embarking on this educational journey with me. This book is the culmination of countless lessons and insights gained over the years, refined, and tailored to support teaching multilingual learners.

I hope this book has served as a valuable guide, inspiring you to explore the depth and beauty of language, culture, and identity. May it encourage critical thinking and highlight the transformative power of languages as you and your students engage in meaningful dialogue and self-discovery through explicit cross-linguistic instruction.

Education is inherently political. Biliteracy education in the U.S. has not always been guided by facts, data, or solid research. In my experience, biliteracy advocates have often been marginalized and silenced. Policymakers shape seasons of equity, access, and privileged pedagogy; while the full embrace of bilingual education is evolving, it is yet to be fully realized. Therefore, expanding cross-linguistic transfer instruction has been a long journey. Creating an academic space where English and Spanish can coexist and be connected, compared, contrasted, and developed is an ongoing process.

Today, there is a compelling argument for biliteracy centered around cultural and linguistic communication in the context of globalization, fueled by mass media. Multilingual and multicultural competencies are now at the forefront of educational reforms, offering a deep sense of reassurance and hope.

As you continue this journey, may you do so with courage, enthusiasm, passion, and compassion. Your role as an educator is vital to society, democracy, and global understanding. Know that your efforts and contributions are deeply appreciated and indispensable.

Thank you for your dedication and commitment to expanding the joy and advantages of multilingualism and multiculturalism.

With gratitude and best wishes,

–Silvia Dorta-Duque de Reyes

References

Ada, A. F. (1990). *A magical encounter: Latino children's literature in the classroom*. Santillana USA.

Ada, A. F. (2016). *Todo es canción: Antología poética*. Santillana USA.

Ada, A. F. (2023). Ser como tú in *FARO Set IV—Suggested grade levels 3–4*. Velázquez Press.

Ada, A. F., & Campoy, F. I. (2003). *Esta linda la mar*. Santillana USA.

Ada, A. F., & Campoy, F. I. (2010). *Spanish literacy: Strategies for young learners*. Frog Street Press.

Ada, A. F., & Campoy, F. I. (2018). *Palabra amiga*. Velázquez Press.

Ada, A. F., & Campoy, F. I. (2020). *La fascinante historia de la lengua española*. Velázquez Press.

Ada, A. F., & Campoy, F. I. (2023a). *El encuentro mágico*. Velázquez Press.

Ada, A. F., & Campoy, F. I. (2023b). *La lectura creadora*. Velázquez Press.

Anderson, L., & Krathwohl, D. (Eds.) (2001). *A taxonomy for learning, teaching, and assessing: A revision of Bloom's taxonomy of educational objectives, complete edition*. With contributing authors Airasian, P., Cruikshank, K. A., Mayer, R. E., Pintrich, P., Raths, J., & Wittrock, M. C. Addison Wesley Longman.

August, D. A., Calderón, M., & Carlo, M. (2002). *Transfer of skills from Spanish to English: A study of young learners* [Report for practitioners, parents and policy makers]. Center for Applied Linguistics. https://www.cal.org/acquiringliteracy/pdfs/skills-transfer.pdf

Baumann, J. F., Kame'enui, E. J., & Ash, G. E. (2003). Research on vocabulary instruction: Voltaire redux. In J. Flood, D. Lapp, J. R. Squire, & J. M. Jensen (Eds.), *Handbook of research on teaching the English language arts* (2nd ed., pp. 752–785). Lawrence Erlbaum Associates.

Beeman, K., & Urow, C. (2012). *Teaching for biliteracy: Strengthening bridges between languages*. Brookes Publishing.

Bialystok, E. (2007). Cognitive effects of bilingualism: How linguistic experience leads to cognitive change. *International Journal of Bilingual Education and Bilingualism, 10*(3), 210–223.

Bolaños Cuéllar, S. (2007). Source language text, parallel text and model translated text: A pilot study in teaching translation. *Forma y Función,* (20), 225–252.

Brooks, N. (1968). Teaching culture in the foreign language classroom. *Foreign Language Annals, 1*(3), 204–217.

Bruner, J. (1960). *The process of education.* Harvard University Press.

Bruner, J. (1966). *Toward a theory of instruction.* Harvard University Press.

Campoy, F. I., & Howell, T. (2016). *Maybe something beautiful: How art transformed a neighborhood.* Houghton Mifflin Harcourt.

Carlisle, J. F. (1995). Morphological awareness and early reading achievement. In L. B. Feldman (Ed.), *Morphological aspects of language processing* (pp. 189–209). Lawrence Erlbaum Associates.

Cejas, S., Dorta-Duque de Reyes, S., & Mora, J. K. (2018). The value of contrastive analysis. In S. Dorta-Duque de Reyes (Ed.), *Sound-spelling transfer kit.* Benchmark Education. https://www.benchmarkeducation.com/all-series/sound-spelling-transfer-kit.html

Clemens, N., Solari, E., Kearns, D. M., Fien, H., Nelson, N. J., Stelega, M., Burns, M., St. Martin, K., & Hoeft, F. (2021, December 14). *They say you can do phonemic awareness instruction "in the dark," but should you? A critical evaluation of the trend toward advanced phonemic awareness training* [Research report]. https://osf.io/preprints/psyarxiv/ajxbv

Conti, G. (2015, June 7). *Parallel texts – How they can enhance learning and effectively scaffold reading proficiency development.* The Language Gym. https://gianfrancoconti.com/2015/06/07/870/

Corallo, C., & McDonald, D. H. (2002). *What works with low-performing schools: A review of research*. Roman & Littlefield Education.

Cummins, J. (1978). Bilingualism and the development of metalinguistic awareness. *Journal of Cross-Cultural Psychology, 9*(2), 131–149.

Cummins, J. (1981). The role of primary language development in promoting educational success for language minority students. In C. F. Leyba (Ed.), with California State Department of Education, Office of Bilingual Bicultural Education, *Schooling and language minority students: A theoretical framework*. (3rd ed., 2005, pp. 3–49). Evaluation, Dissemination and Assessment Center, California State University. files.eric.ed.gov/fulltext/ED249773.pdf (pp. 16–62).

Cummins, J. (2021). *Rethinking the education of multilingual learners: A critical analysis of theoretical concepts*. Multilingual Matters.

Deacon, S. H., & Kirby, J. R. (2004). Morphological awareness: Just "more phonological"? The roles of morphological and phonological awareness in reading development. *Applied Psycholinguistics, 25*(2), 223–238. https://doi.org/10.1017/S0142716404001110

Dorta-Duque de Reyes, S. (2005, March 16–19). *Building biliteracy: Organizing instruction for cross-linguistic transfer* [Paper presentation]. California Association for Bilingual Education (CABE) Conference, Los Angeles, CA, United States.

Dorta-Duque de Reyes, S. (2024, February). *The Spanish-English connection: The dynamics of cross-linguistic transfer instruction* [Paper presentation]. National Association for Bilingual Education Conference, New Orleans, LA, United States.

Dorta-Duque de Reyes, S., & Mora, J. K. (2011). *Language subsystems: A framework for contrastive analysis* [Paper presentation]. La Cosecha Conference, Santa Fe, NM, United States.

Escamilla, K. (2000, April 19–20). *Bilingual means two: Assessment issues, early literacy and Spanish-speaking children*. Research Symposium on High Standards in Reading for Students from Diverse Language Groups: Research, Practice & Policy. U.S. Department of Education, Office of Bilingual Education and Minority Languages Affairs (OBEMLA).

Escamilla, K., & Hopewell, S. (2019). Strengthening biliteracy through translanguaging pedagogies. *Bilingual Research Journal, 42*(2), 133–150.

Escamilla, K., Hopewell, S., Butvilofsky, S., Sparrow, W., & Soltero-Gonzáles, L. (2014). *Biliteracy from the start: Literacy squared in action* (Reprint ed.). Brookes Publishing.

Ferreiro, E. (2002). *Alfabetización teoría y práctica.* (5th ed.) Siglo Veintiuno Editores.

García, O., Johnson, S. I., Seltzer, K., & Valdés, G. (2017). *The translanguaging classroom: Leveraging student bilingualism for learning* (pp. v-xix). Brookes Publishing.

Grosjean, F. (1989). Studying bilinguals: Methodological and conceptual issues. *Bilingual Language and Cognition, (1)*2, 131–149.

Hall., E. T. (1966). *The hidden dimension.* Anchor Books.

Hasbrouck, J., & Tindal, G. (2017). *An update to compiled ORF norms* (Technical report No. 1702). Behavioral Research and Teaching, University of Oregon. https://files.eric.ed.gov/fulltext/ED605146.pdf

Heick, T. (2014, February 14). Promoting a culture of learning. Edutopia. http://www.edutopia.org/blog/promoting-a-culture-of-learning-terry-heick

Howard, E. J., Lindholm-Leary, K., Rogers, D., Olague, N., Medina, J., Kennedy, B., Sugarman, J., & Christian, D. (2018). *Guiding principles for dual language education* (3rd ed.). Center for Applied Linguistics.

Irvin, J. L. (1990). Vocabulary knowledge: Guidelines for instruction. What research says to the teacher. *The Reading Teacher, 43*(9), 662–667.

Kroll, J. F., & Bialystok, E. (2013). Understanding the consequences of bilingualism for language processing and cognition. *Journal of Cognitive Psychology, 25*(5), 1–21.

Leonet, O., Cenoz, J., & Gorter, D. (2020). Developing morphological awareness across languages: Translanguaging pedagogies in third language acquisition, *Language Awareness, (29)*1, 41–59.

Levine, D. U., & Lezotte, L. W. (2003). Effective schools research. In J. A. Banks & C. A. McGee Banks (Eds.), *Handbook of research on multicultural education* (pp. 525–547). Jossey-Banks.

Lewis, G., Jones, B., & Baker, C. (2012). Translanguaging: developing its conceptualisation and contextualisation. *Educational Research and Evaluation, 18*(7), 655–670.

Lindholm-Leary, K. J., & Molina, R. (2000). Two-way bilingual education: The power of two languages in promoting educational success. In J. V. Tinajero & R. A. DeVillar (Eds.),*The power of two languages: Effective dual-language use across the curriculum* (pp. 163–174). McGraw Hill.

Linquanti, R., & Hakuta, K. (2012, July). *How next-generation standards and assessments can foster success for California's English learners* (Policy brief 12–1). Policy Analysis for California Education. http://www.wested.org/online_pubs/resource1264.pdf

Machado, A. (2022). *Al maestro Rubén Darío.* Biblioteca Virtual Miguel de Cervantes. https://www.cervantesvirtual.com/nd/ark:/59851/bmc1158178

Mandela, N. (2011). *Nelson Mandela by himself: The authorized book of quotations.* Pan Macmillan.

Minicucci, C., Berman, P., McLaughlin, B., McLeod, B., Nelson, B., & Woodworth, K. (1995). School reform and student diversity. *The Phi Delta Kappan, 77*(1), 77–80.

Montecel, M., & Cortez, J. (2002). Successful bilingual education programs: Development and the dissemination of criteria to identify promising and exemplary practices in bilingual education at the national level. *Bilingual Research Journal, 26*(1), 1–21.

Mora, J. K. (2001). Learning to spell in two languages: Orthographic transfer in a transitional Spanish/English bilingual program. In P. Dreyer (Ed.), *Raising scores, raising questions.* Claremont Reading Conference 65th Yearbook (pp. 64–84). Claremont Graduate University.

Mora, J. K. (2016). *Spanish language pedagogy for biliteracy programs.* Montezuma Publishing.

Mora, J. K., & Dorta-Duque de Reyes, S. (in press). *Biliteracy and cross-cultural teaching: A framework for standards-based transfer instruction in dual language programs.* Brookes Publishing.

National Research Council and Institute of Medicine (1997). *Improving schooling for language-minority children: A research agenda* (D. August & K. Hakuta, Eds.). The National Academies Press. https://doi.org/10.17226/5286

Ramírez, A., & Larrea-García, J. A. (2015, November 4–7). *A descriptive framework for integrating fluency, comprehension, and cognate awareness for emergent to advanced bilinguals* [Paper presentation]. La Cosecha: 20th Annual Dual Language Conference, Albuquerque, NM, United States.

Reyes, P., Scribner, J. D., & Scribner, A. P. (Eds.). (1999). *Lessons from high-performing Hispanic schools: Creating learning communities.* Teachers College Press.

Slavin, R. E., & Calderón, M. (2001). *Effective programs for Latino students.* Lawrence Erlbaum Associates.

Solano-Flores, G., & Trumbull, E. (2003). Examining language in context: The need for new research and practice paradigms in the testing of English-language learners. *Educational Researcher, 32*(2), 3–13.

Thonis, E. (1983). *The English-Spanish Connection.* Santillana USA.

Thonis, E. (2005). *The English-Spanish Connection.* Santillana USA.

Weaver, G. R. (2013). *Intercultural relations: Communication, identity, and conflict.* Pearson.

Wiggins, G. (2012, January 11). *Transfer as the point of education.* Authentic Education. https://authenticeducation.org/transfer-as-the-point-of-education

Yopp, R. H., & Yopp, H. K. (2007). Ten important words plus: A strategy for building word knowledge. *The Reading Teacher, 61*(2), 157–160.

"This invaluable resource empowers students from diverse linguistic backgrounds to connect, collaborate, and thrive, fostering a community enriched with understanding and social growth. A brilliant process for success in multilingual education."

—F. Isabel Campoy

North American Academy of the Spanish Language

"With a strong emphasis on equity and cross-linguistic transfer, Silvia's book is an essential read for educators striving to harness the full linguistic potential of every student!"

—Jacobo R. Izela

Senior Director, Multilingual Education
and Global Achievement (MEGA) Department,
San Diego County Office of Education

"Once again Silvia Dorta-Duque de Reyes, a true maestra in every sense of the word, has expertly guided instructional excellence through a thorough examination of how biliteracy pedagogy can be better framed and taught."

—Jorge Cuevas Antillón

Adjunct Faculty Lecturer, College of Education,
San Diego State University

"Bilingual and dual-language teachers across the country have been calling for more information and guidance around cross-linguistic instruction. Silvia Dorta-Duque de Reyes has answered that call with this excellent teacher's guide. Teachers will find this resource extremely helpful!"

—Rebecca Blum Martinez, Ph.D.

Professor Emerita, University of New Mexico

"Dorta-Duque de Reyes has consolidated knowledge and practices in her work over the years to provide this valuable resource for teachers to leverage cross-linguistic practices and strategies in Spanish and English biliteracy settings."

—Magaly Lavadenz, Ph.D.

Leavey Presidential Endowed Chair in Ethics and Moral Leadership
Executive Director, Center for Equity for English Learners,
Director, Bilingual/Bicultural Education,
School of Education Loyola Marymount University